ON MODERATION

ON MODERATION

Defending an Ancient Virtue in a Modern World

Harry Clor

BAYLOR UNIVERSITY PRESS

Cover Design: Steve Scholl, WaterStone Agency
Book Design: Ellen Condict

Library of Congress Cataloging-in-Publication Data

Clor, Harry M., 1929-
 On moderation : defending an ancient virtue in a modern world / Harry Clor.
   p. cm.
 Includes bibliographical references and index.
 ISBN 978-1-60258-155-5 (pbk. : alk. paper)
 1. Political science--Philosophy. 2. Political ethics. 3. Moderation--Political aspects. I. Title.

 JA71.C56 2008
 320.01--dc22
                            2008010611

Printed in the United States of America on acid-free paper with a minimum of 30% pcw recycled content.

For Margaret, Kate and Laura—loveable exemplars
of moderation

CONTENTS

A<small>CKNOWLEDGMENTS</small>

It would be quite difficult to identify for appropriate recognition every contributor to my thoughts and rumination regarding a subject that has been on my mind for so many years. Here I acknowledge the most direct or substantial contributions.

My colleague Fred Baumann analyzed early drafts with great care, commenting incisively upon weaknesses and raising questions I had left unexplored. No doubt deficiencies remain, but fewer of them than would have existed without Fred. My colleague Kirk Emmert also read this manuscript thoughtfully and offered useful suggestions that I have acted upon. Moreover, I am the beneficiary of Kirk's persistent interest in and encouragement of the project. These specific acknowledgments cannot convey everything that is owed to my friends, including the effect upon me of innumerable lively conversations over the years on subjects related to moderation and immoderation in political and moral life. I also wish to thank Professor Pamela Jensen for many such conversations, and I appreciate the indispensable work of Jalene Fox in preparation of the manuscript. My friend and counselor Jack Finefrock has been extremely helpful with regard to publication considerations. Finally, this book has benefited greatly from the insightful attention lavished upon it by Casey Blaine of Baylor University Press. Casey's editorial work exemplifies that rare combination of stringent expectation and genial inspiration that is the hallmark of a fine editor.

As for long-term influences upon this project, it is important to recognize my teacher and revered mentor, the late Herbert Storing. As Herb's students well know, he was a model of intellectual integrity and of the virtues that moderation can embody. And to my wife Margaret, who has been so supportive in this and other literary ventures, and so tolerant of my (sometimes immoderate) moods, I am more appreciative than it is possible to express in a few, or even in many, words.

INTRODUCTION

We use the term "moderation" and its surrogates all the time in various contexts but not often very reflectively. These essays endeavor to focus on moderation as a concept in such a way as to promote reflectiveness about what it means and why we should care about it. The expression "moderation in all things, including moderation" attaches an ironic witticism to a standard cliché. There is a case to be made that discoverable realities underlie both the cliché and the witticism, though these realities are not so easily manifested as I thought they were when this inquiry first began. As it turns out, making the case involves a long journey through some intellectual terrain that is more recalcitrant and more labyrinthine than one might suppose, and a defense of moderation requires extended engagement with viewpoints contrary to it and claims that can be made against it. Some observers might think that the example presented by horrific contemporary terrorism settles the case against immoderation, but recognition of this evil can serve only as preface to a long inquiry.

In political contexts, superficial usage of the terms "moderate" and "extreme" comes most easily when our observation is confined to current circumstances; that is, to particular situations, issues, and personalities in the forefront of public attention. (For example, right now former

Supreme Court Justice Sandra Day O'Connor is portrayed as a moderate simply because of her supposedly pragmatic inclination to split the difference between the more conservative and the more liberal justices who happened to be on the court at the same time.) I will indicate early on how, more often than not, circumstantial judgments of the sort we so frequently make are ephemeral, incoherent, or confusing.

My project at its outset was to see how far we can get beyond the transient and the parochial. What can be said about the meaning of moderation in *general* terms—that is, in terms generally applicable to human affairs and well-being? The main purpose of these essays is to articulate a coherent, defensible case for moderation as a virtue, the possession and encouragement of which is important for us. But this purpose does not encompass all that they are trying to do. I am also interested in identifying and exploring the various issues, some of them large questions, that arise in the process of justifying moderation broadly and analytically. The largest questions are of course those of moral, psychological, ultimately philosophic import, and these are such as to demand inquiry about facets of human nature; you cannot deal seriously with this subject for long without encountering claims and counterclaims about the wants or qualities that characterize us as human beings. This project thus eventually touches matters much reflected upon by thinkers both penetrating and diverse, including Aristotle, Nietzsche, Freud, Rousseau, and Montaigne. I will not do full justice to these thinkers but will comment at length upon those aspects of their ideas that bear directly on our topic. As this brief and incomplete list of eminent names suggests, there are sizeable controversies to be faced here. Adding to the controversial is the fact that religious viewpoints become relevant, and almost mandatory, to consider at some stages of the argument; hence, certain biblical orientations must be up for discussion.

Moderation and immoderation can be considered from three vantage points, which are necessarily intertwined but are also diverse as to the problems they pose and the mode of analysis they invite: the vantage points of politics, of moral psychology and of philosophy. And that, roughly speaking, is the division of labor operative in these essays.

The first undertakes to define what moderation and immoderation amount to in political life, and to explicate the several perspectives and insights about public affairs that are associated with these concepts; this is, to a large extent, an exercise in definition. The essay is not designed to engage the fundamental philosophic issues, though for help with the project of definition it does draw upon renowned philosophers of moderation (especially Edmund Burke and Aristotle). A prominent theme is whether a balanced, "centrist" statesmanship is compatible or incompatible with wholehearted devotion to a principle, a cause, an ideal; I argue (with qualifications and cautionary provisos) for compatibility. In addition to questions about statesmanship, our subject encompasses questions about regimes or polities (liberal and communitarian polities, for example) and about pervasive issues in civic affairs (issues concerning liberties and communal restraints, "church and state," the rule of law, etc.). If there are moderate and extremist regimes, what makes them such? Is there such a thing as a "centrist" perspective that can serve to illuminate the perennial controversies?

Yet, while politics often forms the context for concerns we have about the moderate and immoderate, it is hardly the only context within which moderation is of interest to us; it is of equal interest with regard to personal life and interpersonal relations. Therefore, the second essay focuses upon personality and especially upon moral character as a desideratum, and deliberative self-control as a major component of character. Here the argument for moderation must confront alternative views of what constitutes human flourishing, particularly viewpoints I call "irrationalist" (and sometimes "romantic"), which denigrate rationality in favor of passion and disparage a self-restraining type of personality in favor of a self-expressive one. Happiness, they say or imply, has little to do with temperance and everything to do with emotive vitality; for example, do you want to love and be loved only moderately? Since this confrontation of outlooks raises questions about the good or ill health of the psyche, I devote considerable attention to the perspectives of certain modern psychologists.

An effort to arrive at plausible judgments about what is and isn't conducive to human flourishing makes sense if one can suppose that there is such a thing as human well-being about which to make judgments. This basic supposition is challenged and debunked by radical skeptics of the moral relativist and "postmodernist" orientation, according to whom all generalizations about what is good for us as a species are, finally, mere products of one's biased opinions or parochial culture. And moral phi-losophies purporting to ground or justify ethical norms are analytically reduced ("deconstructed") to the status of rationalization in the service of those who hold power or aspire to power. One suspects, plausibly, that this reduction of reasoning to mere rationalization has as its special target norms associated with moderation, political and personal. A defense of moderation thus has to defend reason against this form of irrationalism, and the third essay seeks to do so by subjecting to critical scrutiny the assumptions of the debunkers. In chapter 3, I explore crucial ideas of Nietzsche, which are sources—particularly complicated and interesting sources—for relativism and postmodernism. But the Nietzschean attack upon reason is not the only way in which it can be denigrated philo-sophically; reason is rendered problematic from quite different angles by Rousseau and by the book of Genesis, outlooks requiring attention as relevant to the case for moderation. Finally, Montaigne is a key thinker in this inquiry, since Montaigne's renowned espousal of moderation is an espousal itself suffused with, even motivated by, a kind of ethical and epistemological skepticism. Perhaps moderation and skepticism are not simply adversaries.

It is appropriate to provide some remarks as to how these essays are written—their style and mode of argument. Since everyone nowadays is supposed to have bias, it is appropriate to disclose mine; my bias is that of a practitioner of liberal education at the college level for thirty-five years. You will find periodically in each essay references to the theory and practice of liberal education as related to moderation and its prob-lems; that there is such a relation is one of the secondary points I wish to make on the way to the main points. The education we call liberal takes seriously the classical writings and outlooks as well as the contemporary ones. Classical perspectives can be especially useful with regard to this subject, as their concentration upon enduring questions provides us with some intellectual distance from the partisan opinion and demands of the present moment—and "distancing," I try to show, is a crucial aspect of moderation.

Too, a liberal education presents us with diverse and conflicting view-points so that we may come to appreciate the intricacies of evaluation. These essays seek to do that by considering perspectives adversarial to the idea of moderation, or objections likely to arise at certain junctures in the rationale for it, with sufficient clarity as to enable a reader to discern and grapple with what is controversial. As a result of this procedure, some problems in the case for moderation are exposed, but I am not interested in avoiding the problematic. I am far from supposing that the analyses offered here amount to conclusive proofs resolving all difficulties and precluding all doubts; issues concerning human well-being with which this inquiry has to be involved do not lend themselves to conclusive, once-and-for-all resolution. With a subject of this sort, it seems to me, one doesn't prove things, yet one can make arguments more or less rationally defensible in light of pervasive experiences. Here moral absolutes are very hard to come by; my rationale for moderation has less to do with categorical principles of right and wrong than with happiness and unhappiness. In such an arena, any significant proposition you could assert will be open to questioning from some perspective or other and subject to exceptions in some contexts. But it hardly follows that here there are only subjective opinions—all equally valid because equally unarguable—so that nothing could be said persuasively about the contribution of moderation to our welfare. According to the outlook informing these essays, there are truths to be discovered, but truths complex and many-sided; the best way to get at them is by engaging contrary ideas in a manner approximating dialogue.

As to audience, these essays are not designed to address only professional scholars or political and moral theorists. My intention has been to write them in such a manner as to render them accessible to well-educated persons interested in large questions of human affairs. While I certainly want this work to be relevant to professional analyses and disputations on these matters, I have written it with one eye on the citizen. After all, moderation and extremism are phenomena of widespread interest in academia and in society at large, too. Therefore these essays avoid the more abstract, recondite conceptualizations of the issues; the effort is to clarify. Clarity is sought by frequent references to ordinary experience with the aid of writings (including, by the way, imaginative literature) that help us to reflect upon experience. Liberal education has taught me this mode of procedure. Another way to say all this is that the essays are addressed to those who are in a position to be educators in the broad sense of the term.

One last observation. You might think that the prominence of mass-murdering terrorism in our contemporary world makes the case against immoderation easier to mount and to accept. I do not know if this is so, but I hope that our perception of this most obvious and blatant form of extremism—politically, ethically, religiously—might serve to render us more attentive to the broader considerations with which theorizing about the moderate and the immoderate is concerned and which would still be important if there were no terrorism. In what follows, I do refer to current terrorism for illustrative purposes, but the inquiry is primarily about the enduring considerations. What is moderation in public and personal life, and why should we want it?

Chapter 1

POLITICAL MODERATION
Balancing the Extremes

Moderation is rarely perceived as an exciting subject. Indeed, an author who is excited by the idea, as I am, might be thought a bit eccentric. Yet the concept is of far-reaching import, and an argument on its behalf encounters very interesting dilemmas and faces the risk of platitudinous solutions.

Consider how frequently the terminology of moderation is employed in our discourse about matters political, social, and personal.[1] The idea that there are "moderate," as opposed to "extremist," leaders, movements, policies and regimes is so pervasive that it might seem an inherent or unavoidable premise of our perception and discussion of public issues. Also pervasive is the supposition in much of this discourse that moderate and extremist are discernible realities and that the former is something desirable while the latter is not. Yet we seldom undertake to focus analytically on these judgments—to explore them systematically or consider the grounds of our assumptions about human affairs when we make them. This is unsurprising; such an inquiry is more likely to come up with questions, problems, or anomalies than any simple or clear-cut answer.[2]

Is there a rational basis for regarding some heads of state or movements (political, cultural, religious) as "fanatical," while their adversaries are not so regarded? Perhaps it is all a matter of opinion, political bias, and relativity—cultural or ideological. Extremist compared to what, you might ask, and isn't it the case that "one man's fanatic is another's freedom fighter"? Perhaps the ordinary view that the fanatic is one who acts violently in a wholly irrational manner or for uncompromisable ends amounts to nothing more than a conventional dogma or at best a salutary myth. (Yet if "one man's fanatic is another's freedom fighter" is to be taken literally as a serious proposition, it would follow that mass-murdering suicide bombers are not fanatical, except from the biased emotional perspective of those injured by them or those unappreciative of their "cause.")

This essay is an effort to grapple with the question of rational basis by examining, in serial order, several major conceptions of what political moderation means, considering as we go the vicissitudes of each, and the extent to which each one in particular and the several collectively can be justified.

In ordinary political parlance, the moderate position is usually thought of as a position located between opposite extremes. In other words, a sharp polarity is observed, and an area one deems sufficiently distant from both ends is envisioned as the "center." We find this perspective reflected in journalistic accounts and books on contemporary issues, as well as commonsense observations of the man on the street.[3] This familiar and commonsensical procedure has interesting vicissitudes.

As to the uses of government and the scope of its activity, is President George W. Bush classifiable as a centrist, a middle-of-the-road political figure? Until recently at least, many regarded Bush as such—especially when contrasted, explicitly or implicitly, with a Ted Kennedy on his left and a Newt Gingrich on his right. Yet the latter two can both look moderate if compared to revolutionary socialists on the one hand and right-winged antigovernment militants on the other. Does judgment depend entirely upon what one chooses to identify as the extremes?

Franklin D. Roosevelt certainly did not pursue a course of action nicely intermediate between the liberals and conservatives of his time. His

vigorous leadership carried the nation substantially in a "liberal" direction. The New Deal has been viewed by many (friends and enemies) as
having initiated a near revolution regarding the role of government in the
regulation of economic enterprise, reduction of social inequalities, and
introduction of welfare measures for the less affluent. But from a broader
perspective, FDR's position can be seen as a moderating force—standing
between grave threats from the far left and the far right; the New Deal
reforms were calculated to protect our civic order, democratic capitalism,
from both. Arguably, the liberal welfare state as such is susceptible of
characterization as a "vital center." Which of these two perspectives (if
either) is the more valid or appropriate one?

We could make the case that the latter is of the more historic importance. But then judgment is made to depend ultimately upon what one
regards as the fundamental issues.[4]

The problem of definition is further complicated where political
movements are motivated by religion. Early in the war in Afghanistan,
we heard a proposition that "moderate Talibans" might be acceptable in a
reconstituted regime. Spokespersons for the embattled opposition replied
in effect that this is a blatant oxymoron; Talibans are necessarily extremists. Not too long ago some Saudi Arabian leaders expressed the hope
that a trend toward moderation would gradually come to prevail in that
country's Islam. What could they (supposedly Wahabi Muslims or their
supporters) mean by religious moderation? And how is the concept at all
applicable to religion or religiously inspired movements?

Hence critics have various opportunities to argue that "moderate"
and "extremist" are phenomena wholly subjective and situation-bound,
utterly dependent upon variable opinions or commitments, circumstances and partisan perceptions of circumstances (ephemera like the
shifting shadows in Plato's cave). So what sense does it make to take
the concept seriously as applying to things real and important? At this
stage of the inquiry, perhaps the most one can say affirmatively is that
pragmatically situational judgment calls may be defensible in view of our
particular concerns here and now. (For example, some of Bush's policies
can be seen as occupying periodically a kind of middle ground regarding
domestic matters at issue these days, and right now the term centrist is
applied to Ariel Sharon's policy concerning a Palestinian state.) But this

is unsatisfying; those of us unsatisfied with it must search for a reasonable way to think of the subject trans-situationally, that is, in terms of *attitudes* and *outlooks* having more enduring import. And we are obliged to consider more systematically why it makes sense to evaluate political moderation positively, as something beneficial. The negative evaluation may be summarized as follows:

Moderate can only mean a disposition to tepid, middling compromise between opposing ideals. Moderation is a weakness, a timid unwillingness to take a clear and decisive stand, a mere utilitarian "splitting of the difference." It is the opposite of what matters and is admirable—principled and wholehearted commitments. It is mediocrity at variance with greatness, which entails passionate devotion to a cause, therefore an inevitable one-sidedness.

A reply can be made that moderation is not simply a matter of being in the middle of whatever (perceived) extremes happen to be around. The moderate politician builds consensus and unifies; he or she seeks agreement across partisan lines and speaks to the people in a nonconfrontational, noninflammatory way intended to be unifying. This perspective gets us a bit beyond a mere splitting-of-the-difference. But consensus is often unenduring; there is a distinction to be made between an ephemeral and a deep-seated, long-term consensus. Nor is a widely shared opinion always the most desirable outcome; we can envision such a thing as a widely shared opinion that is unjust, even "extremist." And speaking softly and soothingly is not at all times what is indicated; spirited rhetoric can be essential for effective leadership (e.g., FDR's "rendezvous with destiny"). And confrontational pronouncements might be the thing most needed (e.g., Theodore Roosevelt against "malefactors of great wealth," Churchill against the Nazis and their appeasers, and, for that matter, Bush on the "war on terrorism").

It would seem that moderation is noninflammatory and harmonizing only sometimes—or, alternatively, that it is praiseworthy only sometimes. Paradoxically, perhaps, if we are to get beyond loose generalities of this sort, we need to gain some intellectual distance from particulars familiar to us, yet ambiguously many-sided. The inquiry should move for a time to higher theoretical levels—and hence to identification of the recurrent political questions and problems on account of which moderation is of perennial importance.

Once while teaching a course on the American Founding I thought it appropriate to stress the virtues of political moderation. An outstanding student (and congenital debunker) responded with a challenge: "So you would have been against the American Revolution or you would have looked for some compromise to avoid it!" At the time the question threw me embarrassingly off balance.

An article by the late Martin Diamond comes partly to the rescue; the article is entitled "The Revolution of Sober Expectations."[5] The idea is that, in contrast to other revolutions—the French and Bolshevik ones, for example—the American Revolution was tempered by relatively limited aims or aspirations that are inconducive to terror and tyranny. This contrast is illustrative, and worthy of reflection with a view to my project here.

The Declaration of Independence did not declare, as the Communist Manifesto did, that its "ends can be attained only by the forcible overthrow of all existing social conditions."[6] Communist revolution must demand the forcible overthrow of the entire social order because of its all-encompassing ends: the total abolition of private property and thus economic conflict, the transformation of social relations motivated by private advantage, and the eventual creation of a wholly different, unselfishly communal type of person (the "New Man").[7] Prior to that outcome the radical revolutionary is filled with righteous rage at the world's abominable deficiencies, and he is tempted to use massive violence to replace the reign of abomination with the reign of brotherhood, equality, and justice.

The Declaration of Independence contemplated the use of lethal force, but it did so upon no such grandiose expectations for totalistic change in human relations and personality. Force is to be used, as necessary, for the sake of government by the consent of the governed and certain "inalienable" individual rights which (in their Lockean derivation) are reflections of elementary human interests. Of course, these principles are important, and their institutionalization necessarily entails significant social changes; however, they neither presuppose nor require the wholesale reconstruction of our motivations and relations so as to achieve the vision of a thoroughly communalized world. More precisely, the work of the American Founders leaves private property intact, along with the self-seeking inclinations associated with property and pursuit of material prosperity. The philosophy of the Founding does not aspire to root out the ultimate causes of economic and social conflict or all the inequities, even vices, that arise from factional ambitions. Rather, as is well known, the worst outcomes are to be prevented by the mutual checking and balancing of such interests and ambitions. The ultimate causes are thought to be "sown in the nature of man" and beyond reach, short of despotic means. These aspects of the American polity can serve to supply us with one model of political moderation.[8]

A number of inferences might be drawn from the antithesis between this model and communism. The one I want to draw is that moderation can be seen as a realistic limitation of aspiration as to what can be accomplished politically, even at the highest level of constitution-making. Moderation is a recognition of limits, the adversary of what we may call "transformationalism" or "maximalism." It views as dangerously utopian, and conducive to virulent strife, any grand scheme to impose on actual human beings (as distinguished from the characters in literary or theoretical utopias) a social order flawlessly just or morally pure. The moderate political leader or citizen might be a reformer, but the reforms will be tempered with cognizance that, on account of human frailties, the possibilities for benign innovation are far from boundless. This outlook cultivates a willingness to put up with some defects in institutions—even some evils in government and society—on the premise that they cannot be eradicated, or from the perception that a thoroughgoing effort to eradicate them threatens to unleash greater vices and evils. Political moderation is informed by a cautionary skepticism (articulated or unarticulated) about our prospects for institutionalizing, or otherwise causing to be socially predominant, our ideal visions of the good life. It serves then to counteract the rage to which maximalists are given when ideals are unrealized.

You might want to say that this is a standing invitation to complacency and that the bounds of realistic aspiration are variable; they are different in different times and places. Is the perception of limits that seems to characterize moderation nothing more than commonly accepted perceptions of existing conditions which only appear to be stubborn facts of life? (Perhaps the American Founders mistook the commercialism and factionalism of their times for such stubborn facts.) Proponents of political moderation must acknowledge that awareness of and accommodation to longstanding historical or habitual constraints is a large part of what it is about, as adamant refusal to recognize such constraints is a certain kind of "extremism." But often underlying such an acknowledgment one can discern a claim that there are limitations, ultimate and permanent, arising from the human condition—the kind of beings that we are naturally. Prominent among these is the pervasively observable fact that most of us most of the time are self-interested beings with basic desires to stay alive, maintain material well-being, and experience more pleasure than pain. Also prominent is a propensity to exercise power when occasions allow,[9] and the associated disposition to pride or vanity by which, among other things, one seeks to beautify these inclinations with moral rationalizations or humanitarian pretenses. (Apparently we are the only animals who can deceive ourselves.) To be sure, these are not the only aspects of man's nature that are relevant to our subject. But the denial of them and conviction that human beings are wholly malleable is a standing invitation to political maximalism. Insofar as these are pervasive human inclinations, they constitute, collectively, one of the major reasons that there are no flawless solutions—even moderate ones—to our social problems.

Here is a third concept of political moderation closely associated to the one just considered but giving rise to some different questions. It remains to be seen how far this concept is dependent on the same view of human nature as its predecessor. In definition of true statesmanship, Edmund Burke writes, "We compensate, we reconcile, we balance. We are able to unite into one consistent whole the various anomalies and contending principles that are found in the minds and affairs of men."[10] The root idea here is that there are always diverse and competing desiderata in political life, and that this reality determines the fundamental task of statesmanship, that of balancing and reconciling. This is not simply a recognition of persistent conflict (Marxists do that, and so do fascists and radical

Islamists). Nor is it only factional "interests" in the Madisonian sense that are in contention. The point is that, in many cases, each of the opposing demands you have to deal with reflects a *principle* deserving of your consideration as an aspect of the public good. Immoderation is characterized by a one-sided or absolute commitment to a good that is in fact only one good among several. (Burke accused the French Revolutionaries of maximizing populistic equality at the expense of civic order, property, and morality or decency.) The balancing enterprise characterizing moderate statesmanship necessarily encounters "anomalies" because you are fighting on behalf of standards of value that may be in contradiction. Accordingly, while this statesmanship is not identifiable simply with resolute devotion to a cause, it is surely distinguishable from an unprincipled avoidance of commitment. Its real practitioner cannot be someone intellectually or morally mediocre; it requires certain virtues of mind and character—the wisdom, the seriousness, and the courage to come to grips with intricacies or ambiguities, ethical as well as tactical, concerning matters of far-reaching import.

Looked at from this viewpoint, moderation in politics has something in common with thoughtful scholarship, which has to take disinterested account of opposing perspectives on a complex question. In the former case, however, action is required, and here our viewpoint encounters one of the more interesting objections to it. A leader—for that matter, anyone—who is too keenly aware of the weighty considerations "on all sides of the question" will find it difficult to take a definite position and maintain it vigorously. Perhaps there is such a thing as too much open-mindedness (or too much of what some contemporary liberals call "value pluralism"). Excessive cognizance of competing claims may lead to a relativistic outlook that paralyzes action or induces drift to an unprincipled middle. As Montaigne remarks, "You get lost considering so many contrary aspects and diverse shapes."[11] As Hamlet, that famous intellectual waverer, puts it, you can become "sicklied o'er with the pale cast of thought." The danger is familiar to many intelligent people, including those involved in the enterprise of liberal education, where students and educators are compelled to confront contrasting doctrines presented by thoughtful proponents. Perhaps intellectual paralysis is, for a time, a good thing in education, but political paralysis, where there are great causes at stake, is not. Should we say, with Nietzsche, that wholehearted belief is the prime condition of resolute action, and that the condition of wholehearted belief is that you live under a kind of "veil" that screens out much of the world's moral diversity?[12] This line of argument is bad news for the concept of moderation, yet history furnishes some impressive counterexamples testifying for the proposition that political moderation is compatible with action both principled and resolute.

As a model, the conduct and character of Abraham Lincoln come quickly to mind. In his debates with Stephen Douglas and his presidential campaign of 1860, Lincoln stood on a platform of "no extension of slavery" whatever into the Territories. He did not propose to abolish slavery at that time in the states where it already existed. The position is two-pronged: the policy of "no extension" reaffirmed the principle that slavery is a wrong (the Declaration of Independence being right), and the compromise with it in the existing southern states was thought necessary to save the Union from dissolution.[13] Lincoln can thus be seen as occupying a middle ground between abolitionists and supporters of the southern cause. Now Stephen Douglas may also be seen as occupying a middle ground; his policy of allowing local majorities in the Territories to decide the controversy for themselves was offered as a Union-saving measure (by taking the inflammatory issue out of national controversy), and he apparently thought that this local "popular sovereignty" would eventually lead to the demise of slavery nationally. Do we have to conclude that both Lincoln and Douglas were the moderate statesmen on this great controversy? To an extent I think we do, but Lincoln has the greater claim to that title. More clearly than Douglas, Lincoln squarely confronted and wrestled with the two crucial imperatives: fundamental human equality and preservation of the republican Union. As to the former, Lincoln adamantly rejected all compromises with the principle of "no extension"; he would not tolerate even seemingly small concessions on the issue of extension.[14] And he conducted the politics of the war with a view to eventual emancipation *and* eventual reunion. One can hardly regard as unexciting utilitarian mediocrity Lincoln's relentless efforts to balance and fulfill these two vital imperatives of his time; consider the intense pressure to which he was subjected by righteous opinion from all sides. That in this endeavor he had to make agonizingly difficult, even ethically distasteful, choices and compromises seems only to highlight the impressiveness of Lincoln's characteristic fortitude and self-control. (It would seem the easier, less demanding course to take a categorically abolitionist position like that of Emerson and Thoreau, especially when one has no political responsibility for the consequences.) The problem of resolute action in the face of competing principles can hardly be resolved by one historical illustration, but the case of Lincoln does serve to exemplify this frequently unrecognized truth: moderation and greatness are not opposites.[15]

Let us return to our more-or-less Burkean definition, which associates political moderation with a deep awareness of the plurality of goods and ends (the source of extremism being ignorance or denial of this reality). This plurality is another major reason that there are no flawless political solutions. The conclusion seems unavoidable that where there is an effort to "balance" disparate demands, the resulting arrangement will have to satisfy some at the expense of the others, or it will be a compromise such that all are accommodated partially but none fully. There is no serious balancing without compromise and no compromise without cost, without the sacrifice of something. To state the point a bit differently, in the philosophy underlying political moderation we find the idea that there are antinomies in human affairs and that therefore "you cannot have it all," not ever. One of the most fundamental antinomies I can think of is this: A society seeking to maximize the communitarian side of life, and the thoroughgoing public spiritedness necessary to it (like the old Israeli kibbutz), does so with considerable sacrifice of individual autonomy and the private side of life.[16] On the other hand, a society emphasizing the independence of the individual and encouraging commercial competition (as ours tends to do) cannot normally enjoy strong bonds of national solidarity or expect to have many citizens who care about public affairs as much as they do about private ones. And if you try to institutionalize both of these desiderata you will be unable to satisfy all that is demanded by each. Extremists, communitarian or libertarian, do not know this sort of dilemma or are unbothered by it.[17]

Larger theoretical questions arise. On what basis or premises, after all, do we determine the most vital goods or principles, the ones whose contention imperatively demands the balancing art of statesmanship?

And can one simply settle for plurality? These theoretical concerns should be visited.

I do not see how one could simply settle for plurality—any plurality. (An aggregate of fiercely terrorist groups with different particular objectives, perhaps ethnically derived, might find a leader who can compromise their differences sufficiently so they may terrorize together. Is he therefore a moderate?) If moderation is a rational enterprise, its practitioner must have recourse to an understanding of the desirable or worthy which transcends the particular demands he or she faces, in order to determine which of them, if any, are the essential ones. From what source is such an understanding derivable? For Burke, who denigrates political theory as an invitation to extremism, it is derivable from practical wisdom or prudence about circumstances bearing on the well-being of the country. But this approach implies that even prudence is in need of some vision of a unified good which is more than an aggregate of the contending desiderata (especially if these are to be "united into a consistent whole"). Are we then to identify political moderation, ultimately, with a firm grasp of the common good or public interest of one's particular polity?

Of course, this conclusion presupposes that there is such a thing as the public or national interest, that "what is good for the country" is in some sense an objective or discernable reality. Ultrapluralists and "multiculturalists" would debunk all this as mythology or as matters simply of subjective and diverse opinion. How can there be a common good for a people when they disagree about it and when interests are divergent? Diversity of opinion on the slavery question existed in abundance, yet Lincoln persistently affirmed a national interest on the subject; moreover, a heavy burden of proof rests upon anyone who would debunk Lincoln's view that disunion and abandonment of "government of people, by the people and for the people" and surrender to the proposition that a class of persons is subhuman would amount to real disaster for America. Lincoln thought so on the premise that these principles serve to define us as a country. He also regarded, along with the Founding Fathers, economic prosperity and the opportunity of all to pursue it as essential elements of the country's well-being. But are these things good for America only because it was founded with a view to them—that is, only because of our peculiar history? The problem of diversity and unity among our national interests might be resolved abstractly this way: government by consent of citizens free, equal, and prosperous is what America is unified about. The question remains, however, whether even a valid understanding of one's particular polity is sufficient, or whether by itself it can provide us with an adequate horizon for thinking about what political moderation means.

The most comprehensive point I am obliged to maintain here is two-fold: that certain conflicts of principle and purpose are characteristic of political life per se, and that our thinking about their resolution has to be guided, to a significant degree, by insight about human affairs per se. Are there insights about human affairs as such that are both true and conducive to moderation?

One contemporary liberal philosophy, if valid, could supply the answer. This view, often going by the name of "value pluralism," is that the world we live in (not just the country or culture) presents us with a variety of conflicting goods, values, or ultimate ends that are incommensurable and cannot be ranked in importance by appeal to any standard of the good life transcending them. This conflict is irresolvable; therefore, you have to choose some ultimate ends at the expense of others, and different societies will make different choices. So far the proposition lends itself to these examples: some societies will opt for strong communal bonds over individuality, public over private loyalties, national security over liberty (like contemporary Singapore), or even theocracy over secularism. And who can criticize them for these choices? But such choices are generally disfavored by liberal pluralists. What they end up favoring is a society devoted to accommodating as many of these diverse values and ways of life as possible.

Isaiah Berlin, considered a founding father of this viewpoint, observes, "Pluralism, with the measure of negative liberty [freedom from coercion] that it entails, seems to be the truer and more humane ideal   . . . because it does at least recognize that human goals are many, not all of them commensurable."[18] In a subsequent work, Berlin calls this pluralism "equilibrium." He concludes, "perhaps the best that one can do is try to promote some kind of equilibrium, necessarily unstable, between the different aspirations of different groups of human beings . . . to prevent people from doing each other too much harm, giving each human group sufficient room to realize its own idiosyncratic, unique, particular ends without too much interference with the ends of others."[19] This idea weighs in on the side of political moderation. The society envisioned is far preferable to one in which opposing groups—ethnic, religious, or ideological—exterminate each other in struggles for exclusive control of the state. But what does this polity as such stand for? In brief it stands for the avoidance of grievous "harm" and for toleration of ethical diversity. William Galston, an elaborator of Berlin's perspective, summarizes the problem as follows: "Suffice it to say that if moral pluralism is the most nearly adequate depiction of the moral universe we inhabit, then the range of choiceworthy human lives is very wide. While some ways of life can be ruled out as violating minimal standards of humanity, most cannot. If so, then the zone of human agency protected by the norm of expressive liberty is capacious indeed."[20] Galston's "expressive liberty" means an entitlement to live as you please. Since under this entitlement individuals and groups will please to live very differently, it must follow that tolerance is an underlying—if not *the* underlying—social norm, overriding much else.

Tolerance is not a solution to all problems, as Berlin and Galston seem to recognize when they hedge their affirmations with various qualifications and provisos. Berlin is right to characterize his equilibrium as "unstable." The instability, I think, arises largely from its insufficient provision for civic unity and for a unifying public morality (considerations that are, by the way, prominent on Edmund Burke's list of social necessities). After all, value pluralism is not simply an argument on behalf of our conventional liberal accommodation of diverse ethnicities and religions; it extols moral diversity. On the face of it, value pluralists are offering as a model of the most desirable society the one encompassing disparate ethical standards to the greatest extent possible. This dispensation would impose stringent demands indeed upon the human capacity for toleration. Is it not evident that sharp disagreements on values deemed fundamental to a worthy human life impose much strain on the virtue of tolerance? Of course, toleration is a virtue (of which moderation is in need often enough), and its scope can be fairly extensive

—where underlying it is a widespread consensus on some ethical fundamentals.[21] In other words, tolerance by itself does not produce the sense of community upon which it depends. Some contemporary pluralists seem unaware of this problem; others grapple with it periodically, though rather ambiguously. Where attention is given to requisites of civic attachment or identity, much greater attention is given to the importance of plurality. The attempt is made to preclude ways of life deemed very harmful, though it is not often clear what is encompassed by their concept of "harm." Norms can be maintained against ways of life violating "minimal standards of humanity," such as, say, the practice of human sacrifice, but what about polygamy, sadistic pornography, extremely violent or degrading entertainments, a "drug culture," and the like? And what about public education concerned with promotion of common standards of value, including patriotism? Our value pluralists are generally elusive about such questions, but the main thrust of their doctrine strongly suggests that support for communal bonds would be sparse and the common ethos rather thin.[22]

Beyond these considerations is a philosophic issue raised by the claim that the conflicting goods, or cherished forms of life, in "the moral universe we inhabit" are wholly incommensurable and unrankable. I can accept this far-reaching proposition in part. To distinguish their position from outright relativism, these pluralists maintain (in addition to their acknowledgment of elementary "humanity") that some of the contending goods they have in mind are really good. For example, a life devoted to family and one devoted to country are both humanly worthy lives, though when these commitments are in contention, the contention is irresolvable either by a cost-benefit analysis of utilities or by appeal to some universal standard of right. I agree about the utilitarian cost-benefit analysis; these commitments are not commensurable in the sense that they could be reduced to measurable quantities of the desirable. Neither could the controversy be rationally determined by direct application of a universal principle which would say "Always choose this alternative"; one has to consider the circumstances. But why are we entitled to call both of these lives good ones if there is no recourse to an understanding of human well-being or worthiness as such? What makes them good? Perhaps when we so regard them we have in mind their contribution to the flourishing of a rational and social animal. If so, then this and other antinomies, while not resolvable in any absolute way, are amenable to illumination by reflection on the human condition; that they are antinomies is not the last word to be said about them.

Value pluralism does come down on the side of political moderation but without allowing for sufficiently penetrating consideration of what that requires and what makes it good. This liberal outlook cannot constitute the last word on our subject.

When I search for words synonymous with moderation, the term "proportionality" comes readily to mind. A sense of proportion is appropriate at all levels of politics, but especially so at the highest levels. In *Federalist #37* James Madison noted that a major difficulty encountered by the Constitutional Convention "must have lain in combining the requisite stability and energy in government with the inviolable attention due to liberty and the republican form."[23] The analysis goes on to discuss "the difficulty of mingling them together in due proportions." As the Founders' approach to resolution of this problem is widely known, I will only say this much about it here: The democratic principle of popular sovereignty, if pushed considerably, would require that all significant public offices be elective and that the elections be quite frequent so that agencies of government are maximally responsive to popular inclinations. But this would entail such frequent change of officeholders and such subjection of them to transient opinions as would be incompatible with decisive government and continuity in public policy. The Constitution addressed this dilemma by arranging that the democratic principle should be operative in differing degrees in the several branches of the federal government; the Senate, presidency, and federal courts were distanced in varying degrees from current popular opinions or passions, while the House of Representatives (expected to be powerful) was not distanced. Thus we have a constituted representative democracy, as distinguished from radical populistic democracy.

I have three additional inferences to draw. This arrangement, subject to alterations the Constitution allows, has worked rather well. The antinomy the Constitution-makers encountered is not intractable; it is amenable to alleviations, which, while complex and imperfect, are at the least acceptable. Second, the dilemma here is fundamental; the framers did not think of the disparate considerations they wrestled with simply as two "values" in a pluralistic mix of many goods. The demands of effective government and the demands of political liberty must be reconciled before other goods can be secured. The concern with establishing effective institutions of representative government is prior to concerns we may have about value pluralism or lifestyle diversity. Third, the Founders did not think of the two imperatives as American imperatives only, or of the needed proportion between them as an American interest only. After all, as Constitution-makers, their decisions were no mere reflections of an existing social order; they were in a position to shape that order and in doing so appeal to principles or premises of more universal import. Among these is the premise of the Declaration of Independence that certain natural rights belong to "all men" equally.

The doctrine of natural rights is subject to philosophic dispute or skepticism, and the skeptic would hardly accept that doctrine's premises as *the* transnational horizon for thinking about political proportionality. And it need not be. Edmund Burke was no proponent of the theory of natural rights, or of natural equality, yet as to the character of the principles and purposes whose controversy mandates high statesmanship, Burke's insight is remarkably similar to the Madisonian one.

> To make a government requires no great prudence. Settle the seat of power; teach obedience and the work is done. To give freedom is itself more easy. It is not necessary to guide; it only requires to let go the rein. But to form a *free government*, that is to temper together those opposite elements of liberty and restraint in one consistent work, requires much thought, deep reflection, a sagacious, powerful and combining mind.[24]

Obviously "free" and "government" are identified here as the opposing desiderata most imperatively requiring combination. Indeed, it is strongly suggested that liberty and restraint are the fundamental imperatives of all (not just British) civic life, and that is why their reconciliation is the task at the core of a politics deserving to be called statesmanship. Despite his oft-repeated distaste for theoretical speculations about universals, Burke's thought does yield a proposition of comprehensive import. Against the enthusiastic libertarianism of the French Revolution, he held that restraint upon our passions is as much of a human need as liberty or freedom of choice. Insofar as Burke has an overall conception of the good, it is this: "a moral, regulated liberty" is what is good both for a country and a person.[25]

This is a significant claim, but it is a generality needing to be qualified by the renowned Burkean emphasis upon the centrality of prudential judgment about circumstances. The critical proportion—how much liberty and what kinds of restraints?—cannot be settled upon any abstract or universal principle. The appropriate proportion, depending upon practical wisdom, would be somewhat different for England, France, and America (and, to update, Turkey and Afghanistan, which have intense ethnic and religious antagonisms to address).

The cautionary insight just noted concerning the limitations of theory or abstract principle deserves to be counted among the components of political moderation. Aristotle, also a philosopher of moderation, stresses the importance of the prudential almost as much as Burke does. Aristotle introduces his inquiry about ethical and political norms with a methodological warning as to what we may reasonably expect from any such inquiry. "Our discussion will be adequate if it has as much clearness as the subject matter admits of, for precision is not to be sought for alike in all discussions. . . . Now fine and just actions, which political science investigates, admit of much variety and fluctuation of opinion."[26] The central idea is that exact and universal truths are not to be expected concerning this "subject matter"—moral and political well-being—because of the great variability of the circumstances in view of which judgments of the just and the unjust, the good and the bad, have to be made. A course of action, policy, or pronouncement that is valid in some or most cases would be wrong, even disastrous, in certain situations, and there will be exceptions to any proposition you could affirm. Aristotle does not conclude that there is no truth to be had in this area but rather that assertions must be formulated "roughly and in outline," and the best of them are "only for the most part true."[27]

These following illustrations of the point come to mind: Ethical doctrine cannot provide absolute proscription against lying and killing, because in some situations deception or war will be the preferable option or the lesser of evils. And political science cannot affirm that, always and everywhere, "power tends to corrupt and absolute power corrupts absolutely" (Lord Acton's oft-repeated aphorism). Sometimes power ennobles, and nearly absolute power did not corrupt a Pericles or a Lincoln. One may say, consistently with common sense, that Lord Acton's proposition is for the most part true; power often corrupts and absolute power is very dangerous (if occasionally necessary). The warning against abstract universalization applies at all levels of abstraction, even where generalization is confined to time and place. You might be able to conclude that liberal democracy is the best regime available for contemporary nation-states, but you cannot reasonably conclude that it is best for all of them right now; some nations would be lucky to be ruled by a constitutional monarchy or respectable aristocracy.

The Aristotelian outlook sends two different messages about knowledge and judgment. You can hope to acquire a certain form of knowledge about human affairs generally, based upon experience coherently reflected upon, and defensible ethical judgments can be made. But don't try to turn the study of politics into an exact science, and don't try to turn ethics into a body of categorical imperatives. In the kind of world that these messages presuppose, political moderation is most at home.

In that world, broad principles and ideas can provide guidance for our thinking about what ought to be done but do not by themselves provide any conclusive answers. This consideration needs repeated emphasis, because of a persistent temptation to seek solutions of a political problem by direct imposition of an abstract principle with insufficient attention (in the worse cases, no attention) to the situation's peculiarities. This inclination is sometimes lauded as "idealism," though it might be as much attributable to moral pretense; at any rate, it is usually associated with an erroneously uncomplicated view of the issues and hence the moral alternatives. When obstinately indulged, it gives rise to an excessively doctrinaire or ideological politics rendering compromise and prudential statesmanship virtually impossible. (Consider the abortion issue in the United States, which inadequate leadership has allowed to become a fierce battleground between sharply opposing ideologies that are irreconcilable because each asserts a categorical "right.") Moderation includes an injunction against moralism.

This is an appropriate place to note explicitly that when circumstances change significantly the moderate politician may have to change a policy he has strongly affirmed, thereby running the risk of looking unprincipled. On the other hand he or she might face the charge of extremism when it is necessary to oppose an entrenched political dogma with what might appear to be a contrary extreme (Franklin Roosevelt's case, perhaps). We should test such cases by looking to the statesman's end or purpose; is it concerned with maintaining the balances of the polity?[28]

How do abstract ideas about human life per se appropriately bear upon practical decisions? They cannot do so directly; as previously suggested, their direct application risks dogmatism or worse. They may do so by providing ultimate premises, or intellectual and ethical horizons, within which our thinking about the larger practical issues can be oriented. (The smaller ones are still further from the reach of theory.)

Aristotle's *Ethics* provides us with one thoughtful model of the relations between theory and practice. According to that model, significant observations can be made in general "outline" about the moral life: Ethics is primarily about character (not primarily about binding moral rules). Virtuous character is a set of habitual dispositions to think, feel, and choose in accordance with a mean between opposite extremes, one being an excess and the other a deficiency. In other words, as to passions and actions concerning our well-being, there is always a too-much and a too-little, and ethical reflection can give us a rough general account of these extremities that are to be avoided. Now the proper mean, as Aristotle emphasizes, is always "relative to us" and yet it is amenable to rational consideration. The "relativity" to which Aristotle refers is not a relativity of subjective opinion but of the various situations we confront. So the virtuous course of action cannot be the same thing in all situations, though practical wisdom can provide guidance by illuminating the situation.[29]

The overview that reflection can offer us is best illustrated here by reference to two Aristotelian virtues that are of prominent political importance: courage and good temper. Courage is about our inclinations to fear and confidence in the face of danger. As to fear, the excess of it is what we call cowardice and the deficiency recklessness. The courageous person is not the one who is utterly fearless; there are in the world things to fear. At the time of the Cuban missile crisis, you wouldn't have wanted President Kennedy and his advisors to be recklessly unafraid any more than you would want them to be overwhelmed by fear. The intermediate state of character called courage allows, as the extremities do not, some room for the exercise of sober judgment.

Good temper is a habitual disposition to regulate the natural passion of anger. Unmodified anger or indignation tends to undermine judgment and, in its extremities, gives rise to cruelty and deadly hostilities. (The leading characters in Homer's *Iliad* are driven by rage; so are today's terrorists.) Yet the opposite extreme—no feelings of anger or inability to express them—is an ethical deficiency, for there are things one ought to be angry about (grave injustices, for example). As Aristotle puts it: "For those who are not angry at the things they should be angry at are thought to be fools . . . and unlikely to defend [themselves]."[30] It is easy to see why this subject is of great political import. Political issues, especially large ones, are typically attended and fueled by indignation, more or less ("That's wrong!"), sometimes justified and sometimes not. Aristotle is not one of those who think that because anger or indignation gives us so many problems, it is wisest or healthiest to get rid of it. Like other passions, it has a function to perform in human affairs. Anger, like many of our passions that are the natural raw material of life (pity, sensual desire, pride), is not to be eradicated or simply suppressed but rather controlled and moderated by a habitual self-discipline.[31]

We can plausibly say that every Aristotelian virtue is a form of moderation and is in the service of self-control. Alternative to this comprehensive view of what moderation means is the view famously presented in Plato's *Republic* where it appears among the four cardinal virtues: wisdom, courage, moderation, and justice. This formulation involves a juxtaposition of moderation and courage and invites consideration of possible tension between them. Both of these approaches to the delineation of our subject—the broader or more comprehensive approach and the narrower or more limited mode of definition—find expression in ordinary public discourse, as well as in scholarly literature, and each has its advantages. For purposes of this book I tend to follow the broader model, but do not find it fruitful to adhere to that model with utmost consistency. In some contexts it is necessary to acknowledge virtues or qualities that no definition of moderation can sufficiently account for or encompass (decisiveness in political exigencies, for example). In other words, moderation is of pervasive importance and value in public affairs, but it is not everything. My focus on its pervasive import, with occasional acknowledgment of its limits, is, I believe, in accordance at least with the spirit of Aristotelian moral philosophy.

Aristotelian thought presents us with a kind of "situation ethics," but it is a situation ethics associated with a broad view of human problems and well-being as such. The Aristotelian outlook may be regarded as avoiding two opposite errors in moral philosophizing: dogmatism or absolutism on the one hand and relativism or radical skepticism on the other. This outlook need not be the only model hospitable to the concept of moderation, but it is perhaps the most hospitable. Its supposition is, I believe, that we human beings are sufficiently alike to allow for some comprehensive insights about the welfare of our species, and hence about moderation, but we are far from such uniformity as would permit exact certitudes. The substantial yet flexible ideas of this perspective help us to grapple in a deliberative way with the perennial dilemma of unity and diversity.[32] What is needed is a certain kind of theory which, aware of its limitations, allows us much latitude for pragmatic judgment and intuition.

When we are thinking of the individual, including the statesman, moderation is seen as inextricably associated with self-control. The concept of moderation presupposes both the necessity and the possibility of a kind of self-mastery, and this view depends upon an understanding of the human nature we have in common. But as Plato noted, there is a perplexity here. What is controlling what? That the "I" which masters and the "I"

which is mastered are one and the same is an unintelligible proposition. It must be that some part of me is in control of some other part. The self is divided.

We are, as the old and unrefuted definition has it, rational animals, the former term connoting possession of speech and self-consciousness, therefore the capacity for thought extending well beyond the momentary. But we are also full of imperious passions, some benign and some antisocial, even bestial,[33] which can overwhelm reason and even turn it into their instrument. Then one can become insatiable or fanatical. Self-control means that I am in a position to prevent this from happening, that the thinking part of me retains some degree of authority over the desires or emotions.

This fundamental division in the soul or psyche is at the root of our need for moderation. Keep in mind that the coalition of these disparate elements of our nature is hardly a spontaneous occurrence; it is always a project facing obstacles of some magnitude. Here arises another apparent anomaly regarding self-control: this capacity is almost never achievable on one's own. Its development requires a combination of habituation and enlightenment that is very unlikely to occur without social mandates and institutional norms. We do not become self-disciplined persons without considerable nurture, guidance, and constraints provided by the community or communities in which we live. Elsewhere I have called such communal constraints and institutional norms "public morality."[34] The idea that a public morality is needed would seem a truism, but, when spelled out, it encounters much opposition in liberal modernity. One often encounters the opinion that morality is a private matter. My argument is that the development of character is a matter of vital public as well as private interest. A libertarian might accept this point but insist that desirable ethical norms need no support from public authority; they are sufficiently promoted by "argument, advice and exhortation,"[35] that is, by rational persuasion. It is a pervasively observable fact, however, that the passions do not often follow the dictates of reasoned deliberation alone and unaided by communal standards. We are, to be sure, social beings, but our sociality is in need of much deliberate cultivation.

To elaborate, the perception that we are, at least by classical definition, rational and social beings periodically gives rise to an unduly sanguine vision of the human condition. There is an outlook we may refer to as "rationalism" which supposes that cognitive enlightenment alone, liberated from tradition, religion, and civic bonds, is a power sufficient for the resolution of society's troubles. This outlook is utopian and unsafe. The nonutopian truth is that, for most of us, reason by itself is a rather frail instrument in need of nurture and support from agencies not exactly rational. These include a loving family, a respectable moral or civic tradition (even in the deliberations of the Supreme Court, "precedent" has some authority), and emotionally inspiring rhetoric, symbols, or images ("a picture is worth a thousand words"). In political life the pervasiveness of inspirational rhetoric—even on behalf of the most defensible principles—is testimony to the fact that reason can rarely govern alone.

A similar observation may be made about our natural sociality. It is sanguine complacency to believe that people are by nature social beings in the sense that altruistic impulses can normally be relied upon to outweigh self-centered ones; they cannot. We are such beings in our profound need for social relations; the "I" is deeply in need of a "we." (My cat has no such requirement; neither has it, strictly speaking, a "self.") The human inclination toward union with others is susceptible to, and indeed requires, cultivation by communal norms of various sorts, including some constraints upon the self.

This line of the argument tells half the story. The other half, more easily told and heard in our liberal milieu, has to do with freedom of choice and expression. The ability to make conscious or deliberate personal choices, and the exercise of free will associated therewith, is an essential element of what it means to be a rational agent and to enjoy the dignity thereof. As prominent modern thinkers further maintain, the act of choosing is a crucial energizer of one's higher faculties as well as one's individuality or uniqueness. Where this capacity is suppressed (by an oppressive regime or pervasive social conformity) human faculties are underutilized, hence underdeveloped, and the soul is enervated.[36] From this perspective personal liberty or self-determination becomes the preeminent concern, and any effort by society to impose upon its citizens a far-reaching public morality is destructive of human character because it is destructive of the freedom to decide for oneself how to live.

So here is another apparent antinomy. Self-control is vital for the well-being of a rational animal, but some latitude for self-expression is also vital (literally so; you need it for vitality). Public morality is a desideratum but so is individuality, and each can be carried to an extreme that is harmful because it undermines the other. The point I am making is obvious; here, too, there is need for that disposition to weighing and balancing which characterizes political moderation. The current idea of the autonomous, self-sufficient, private individual inclines toward moral anarchy and is as much a mythology as the collectivist or strongly paternalistic ideologies. These are the "extremists" on this subject. Statesmanlike policy has to seek a delicate balance between the demands of moral unity and the demands of individual freedom of choice. Once again we seem to have a duality of goods to be resolved, case by case as best we can, by informed perception of the existing conditions. (For example, how serious a problem is the current prominence of violent and pornographic entertainments, and what measures can be taken in our social milieu that wouldn't involve more losses in liberty than gains in public decency?)

Can we get beyond such dualities by ultimate appeal to some overarching idea of the good life by which to reflect upon the weightings and balancings? The effort to do so is criticized as "monism."[37] Yet, as I hope this essay has shown, we are hardly able to avoid trying to conceptualize a human good that would give coherence to the diverse goods.

Aristotle calls it "happiness" (in the Greek, *eudaemonia*), which he posits as the final end or "highest good" of all our striving. Happiness for Aristotle is not an aggregate of pleasures; it involves the development or actualization of distinctively human qualities and capabilities (those distinguishing us from other animals). These are the capabilities requisite for living an active life informed by reasoning or deliberation.[38] This is not simply a matter of reasoning; the inclinations, feelings, and emotions of the actualized person are habitually informed by thoughtfulness. One feels, aspires, loves, and gets angry as a rational being. It will come as no surprise that this is a comprehensive yet imprecise definition of happiness. Its imprecision, while considered a defect from some viewpoints, has the advantage that it allows for a variety of means to the end. There are many ways to live a thoughtful life, though not all ways of life would be equally conducive thereto. According to this outlook the exercise of choice regarding how to live is an important ingredient of human fulfillment, but what one chooses is of conclusive import.

There is a modern alternative to this classical view of the *summum bonum*. As noted, Edmund Burke suggests that "a moral, regulated liberty" is what is good for both the community and the person. Tocqueville, that great liberal moderate, teaches that political freedom requires citizens who have "the use of their free will" but have also acquired "habits of restraint." And it is arguable that in the absence of habits of restraint one's choices are hardly choices at all; driven by unregulated desire you can have only preferences. As for the polity, it is an old adage that a licentious people cannot long remain a free people; sooner or later their licentiousness will have to be curtailed by coercive constraints. The paradigmatic idea of a morally and socially tempered freedom takes account of these realities and also of the liberty required for personal and political self-government. In shorthand, the idea of moral liberty can serve as an ultimate point of reference or underlying premise for our thinking about the humanly optimal.[39]

Two reminders are in order here. Since we can think about political moderation transnationally or transculturally to some extent, much can be learned through the study of great exemplars of it from different times and places. I have referred to the American Founders, Lincoln, and Churchill. And, although time will tell, I would like to think that we are seeing in contemporary figures such as Afghanistan's Hamid Karzai the emergence of exemplary moderates in the non-Western world. Much-needed inspiration can be gained from outstanding cases of resolute yet astute confrontation with ideologically charged and dangerous political conflict.

But these very dangerous conflicts remind us of a consideration requiring still more emphasis, lest it be obscured by my emphasis upon the virtues attending political moderation. Since politics inevitably involves the exercise of power in threatening situations, moderation cannot be equated with benevolence or compassion. Nor can it be equated with justice, especially if that means the unconditional observance of cherished moral norms; the moderate statesman knows that sometimes he or she must violate ethical standards which we value and wish to see observed as much as possible. Lincoln, a famously compassionate politician, found it necessary to authorize constitutionally dubious preventive detention of many southern sympathizers; Churchill ordered massive bombings of German cities; Karzai does what he can to stay in power. Sometimes harsh things need to be done, and political moderation therefore is not without its sharp edges.

The concept of statesmanship I have outlined can be clarified by its comparison with two conceptions of political leadership that might be thought similar to it in regard to the morality of politics. The first of these often goes by the name of "realpolitik" or Machiavellianism. Machiavelli advises his "Prince" that "a man who wants to make a profession of goodness in everything must come to ruin among so many who are not good. Hence it is necessary to a prince, if he wants to maintain himself, to learn to be able not to be good, and to use this [knowledge] and not use it according to necessity."[40]

By "good," Machiavelli meant to denote those qualities or standards that are recognized as virtuous in the classical and Christian tradition, along with the conventional norms related thereto. This Machiavellian realism does have some features in common with Aristotelian realism, and it might look like basically the same thing (presented in more striking language)—*if* Machiavelli is interpreted this way: goodness, traditionally understood, is normative, but in certain extreme cases, which present exceptions to the general norm, one must resort reluctantly to immoral means. This is a rather benign interpretation. The more hardboiled and, I believe, accurate interpretation is this: it is a condition of political success that one does not consider oneself at all bound by ethical injunctions or limitations; moral standards should be considered *strategically* as factors in a calculus, to be observed or abandoned as dictated by the "necessity" of the case at hand. Machiavelli asserts:

> This has to be understood: that a prince, and especially a new prince,
> cannot observe all those things for which men are held good, since he
> is often under a necessity, to maintain his state, of acting against faith,

against charity, against humanity, against religion. And so he needs to have a spirit disposed to change as the winds of fortune and variation of things command him, and as I have said above, not depart from good, when possible, but know how to enter into evil, when forced by necessity.[41]

Clearly the clause about not departing from good when possible is hardly the dominant theme of this passage. What is dominant is a picture of political life in which such qualities as faith (that is, abiding by one's promises) and humanity (including abstention from cruelty) are de-normalized. Any close reading of *The Prince* surely reveals that the successful practitioner of great politics is faithless, cruel, and ruthless at least as often—probably more often—than he is reliable, humane, and just, though he will be "a great pretender and dissembler" so as to appear virtuous. This mode of operation is necessary, because in our world of ever-present hostility and danger you cannot maintain your power—and hence the state that depends upon power—otherwise.

Machiavelli has to be credited with discernment of harsh truths, including the harsh truth that falsehood and deception are prominent, even inescapable, factors in political affairs.[42] This theme is pertinent to our subject only insofar as the leader's falsehoods may corrupt his own judgment of reality or are so egregious as to corrupt his followers by turning them into fanatics.

What is more pertinent is the personality of a person who would actually have the capacity to switch one's goodness on and off as variable situations dictate. What kind of person has "a spirit disposed to change as the winds of fortune" do? This utter flexibility would seem incompatible with what we think of as having a character—a set of deep-rooted convictions and more or less habitual dispositions to act in accordance with them. The authentic statesman I have tried to depict must have a character (whatever one's personal defects) that nurtures reliable inclinations to seek and defend a common good. The Machiavellian statesman, who is, we may say, super-adaptable, and hence lacking character in the usual sense, must be both unpredictable and unreliable. Unpredictability might be an advantage against one's enemies, but unreliability is no way to acquire friends.

The crucial distinction between the Machiavellian view of politics and the moderate one is rooted in the disparate visions of the social world underlying them. In Machiavelli's world, ceaseless change and lethal conflict are so predominant as to preclude any moral order at all. Therefore Machiavelli concludes, "I judge indeed that it is better to be impetuous than cautious."[43] On his side one must acknowledge that it is very difficult, as well as unsafe, to try to fight a war moderately. One might wonder whether in cases of dire emergency the concept of moderation has any place at all.[44] Yet there are abundant historical examples of the fact that in war impetuousness can be hazardous, too. What's more, an endeavor to observe certain humane limitations—that is, a kind of cautiousness—is advisable even in times of intense warfare. For this reason, the deliberate slaughter of civilians is generally condemned by civilized nations (or when in extreme exigency this norm is violated it is usually after debate and with professions of regret). And we are not always at war.

Max Weber has offered a conception of political leadership that is concerned with character and which seems to value moderation more than Machiavelli does. In his famous essay "Politics as a Vocation," Weber identifies the authentic possessor of that power-wielding vocation as follows: "One can say that three prominent qualities are decisive for the politician: passion, a feeling of responsibility, and a sense of proportion."[45] By the first of these terms he means passionate devotion to a cause, without which a politician cannot be effective or worthy of respect. Weber appears to demand that this devotion be qualified or balanced by the sense of responsibility and proportion, and he asks an appropriate question: "How can warm passion and cool sense of proportion be forged together in one and the same soul?"[46] This question is of great interest in any effort to understand moderation psychologically. But on attentive reading of Weber it becomes evident that wholehearted commitment to a cause is the vitally conclusive factor, and the other two qualities are ministerial to it; responsibility means assuming responsibility for the success of the cause, and the sense of proportion involves psychological detachment requisite for calculating the consequences of alternative actions with a view to its success. The result of Weberean proportionality is that actions or policies that seem to be identified with one's cherished goal will be rejected when a cool assessment of their probable consequences shows that they would in fact retard it. In other words, one's primary political ends are determined by passionate commitments; the means—that is, the practical exercises of power—are subject to reasoned deliberation. This view of the matter is prominent in modern thought; to what extent is it a formula for moderation?

According to this view, our ultimate ends cannot be judged or shaped by reasoning; what cause a politician ought to pursue is, in the Weberean understanding, "a matter of faith." This is so because "the ultimately possible attitudes toward life are irreconcilable, and hence their struggle can never be brought to a final conclusion. Thus, it is necessary to make a decisive choice."[47] And one's decisive choice has to be dictated by a passion of some sort, there being literally no reason that it should be a moderated choice; it is basically an assertion of will.

This brief account of Weber might be thought at variance with his renowned preference for an "ethic of responsibility" over an "ethic of absolute imperatives." The latter is unconditional, demanding that one do what is (considered) right regardless of predictable results. One of Weber's foremost examples of an absolute ethic is the pacifism of the Sermon on the Mount; it will not allow its devotees to use violence— ever and no matter what. "For if it is said, in line with the acosmic ethic of love, 'Resist not him that is evil with force,'" the pacifist devotee is "responsible for the evil winning out."[48] The authentic politician, recognizing that responsibility, will use as much violence as is necessary to prevent the evil from winning out.

Weberean politics has two features in common with Aristotelian politics. Given the unavailability of categorical or universally valid moral mandates and prohibitions, situational judgment about circumstances becomes crucial. Moreover, the sense of proportion required for such judgment depends, as Weber says, upon a "firm taming of the soul"; this condition of the soul may be regarded as akin to the self-control and balanced perceptiveness characteristic of political moderation. But, as I've suggested, self-control is a complex concept; it matters a lot what aspect of the "self" is doing the controlling or is in the driver's seat.

Finally, the difference between Weberian and classical outlooks outweigh the similarities. The disparity becomes most evident when we ask what, on the former's premises are the "evils" that are to be prevented from winning out. There is no truth discoverable about that question. The Weberian leader does not have available to him for orientation any general understanding of human well-being that is "for the most part true"; what is finally available is only an understanding of the irresolvable clash among diverse versions of what life is about. In this utterly conflicted vision of moral reality, where one's conclusive purposes must be at bottom nonrational assertions of will, what actually is the status of moderation? Assuming that vision, you might want to say that moderation is something real and important, but it is about means, not ends or aspirations. This answer will not do. Unless one subscribes to something like a prohibitive categorical imperative, one's purposes determine the relevant means calculable with a view to their success. If the ends of al-Qaida terrorists cannot reasonably be criticized as fanatically irrational, what sense would it make to judge their cool calculation of the means proportional (conducive) to them as immoderation? (By rigorous calculation, is it more effective to use passenger aircraft or biological weapons to destroy thousands or millions of infidels?)

No doubt that in a thoroughly pluralistic ethical milieu, one could make a decisive choice to observe the limitations I've been calling moderation. By an exercise of will the politician could decide—or decide to believe—that a certain freedom and a certain restraint are both compelling values to be weighted in light of his ultimate value of moral liberty. But why? That would have to be an option for which no argument can be given, and one no more subject to thoughtful evaluation than al-Qaida's choices. In such a world, the proportionate and the moderate, where they can be said to exist, are derivative products of ultimately irrational and unrestrainable commitments.

In his novel *Billy Budd*, Herman Melville depicts his villainous character, John Claggart, this way: He had "apparently little to do with reason further than to employ it as an ambidexter implement for effecting the irrational. That is to say: toward the accomplishment of an aim which in wantonness of atrocity would seem to partake of the insane, he will direct a cool judgment sagacious and sound. These are madmen."[49] I don't mean to suggest that Max Weber or his followers intentionally accommodate such characters, but one fails to find anything in the basic doctrine that clearly makes them ineligible for "the vocation of politics" or provides a real foundation for their denunciation. In the universe Melville envisions, there is apparently a ground for judging some kinds of aims or ends insane and those pursuing them madmen. But standards for this kind of judgment are unavailable in any philosophy that precludes the thoughtful evaluation of one's dominant goals or aspirations.

What about goals and aspirations inspired by religion; to what extent, if any, are these compatible with the concept of political moderation? Consider this rather harsh argument (to which Weber might well subscribe): religious zeal necessarily gives rise to an ethic of absolute imperatives, and resolutely serious religion, at least in its monotheistic and biblical forms, is always zealous. It would not be hard to support this proposition by reference to historic warfare (the Crusades, Catholics vs. Protestants, the murderous jihads) and tyrannical regimes (the Inquisition in Europe, the Mullahs in Iran), all conducted in the name of the Deity and the Deity's awesome commands that the faith be protected or extended. Undeniably such passions have contributed and continue to contribute to many of the world's virulent conflicts.[50] Reading literally from the Sermon on the Mount, Max Weber selected a very different illustration of his claim about religious absolutism: the unconditional Christian demands for peacefulness. Read thusly, the Sermon on the Mount makes no distinction between justified and unjustified fighting; it proscribes fighting and prescribes universal love even for one's mortal enemies. The point here, however, is that sacred texts and movements deal in categorical imperatives, of one content or another, obedience to which must take precedence over any competing worldly considerations. Serious religiosity therefore seems to attack moderation from two opposite directions, creating, from one side, hostilities and strivings for predomination among diverse believers, and, on the other side, piously precluding forceful resistance to dangerous adversaries.

Counterarguments come readily to mind. The sacred texts are not to be grasped with an unreflective literalism; rather they are to be interpreted metaphorically, symbolically, inspirationally. On this kind of premise, Christian philosophers have developed doctrines distinguishing between just and unjust wars and between permissible and impermissible methods of conducting war. Moreover, the numerous theological blessings of peacefulness can be said to perform a moderating function; stringent New Testament injunctions against hatred and anger may be regarded as conducive to the restraint of some of our most ominous propensities. Likewise the condemnation of pride and exaltation of humility can function as antidotes to the diseases of antisocial aggrandizement and despotic inclination.

I will not comment here on the salutary effects these pacific imperatives might have on private interpersonal relations, but, presented by sacred texts in terms apparently absolute, they are rather problematic as to public affairs, often militating (if that is the right word) against prudential political judgment in the face of worldly dangers and evils. It is common knowledge that Gandhi and other influential pacifists resolutely opposed armed resistance to the rise of Nazi and Fascist power. At the time of our missile crisis with Cuba and the Soviet Union, peace demonstrators insisted that the only proper response was to bring the matter before the United Nations for debate. (Our leadership adopted a middle course between entire reliance upon argument and a response so forceful as to hazard escalation toward nuclear war.)

There is a kind of theology that might serve to rescue us from the divergent threats of pious imperialism and antipolitical pacifism to which religious fervor has perennially given rise. It may be summarized as follows. Only God and one's personal relation to God can be absolute; to absolutize anything else, including any political goals or positions, is to be guilty of a form of idolatry. Because one's personal relation to the Deity is so utterly internal and mysterious, it cannot dictate imperatives, on one side or another, of our worldly conflicts. The true believer then does not proselytize, or seek the power to do so, and leaves concerns of the polity susceptible to practical judgment.

Nineteenth-century Christian theologian Søren Kierkegaard may be considered an exemplar of such a view. For Kierkegaard, the Supreme Being or Ultimate Truth is unknowable by us; faith is a "leap in the dark," which one has to take alone in fear and trembling. What authentic faith finally means is a subjective affirmation in the face of radical uncertainty.[51]

This theology is as far from religious warfare as it is from the social gospel. Although the leap of faith has much more to do with passion than with any tempering rationality, it can be said to leave reason intact to wrestle with our sub-eternal social problems unencumbered by religious fervor. The Kierkegaardian believer is not thoroughly irrational; he has a profound awareness that the Infinite is wholly mysterious to us. (One might say that this believer, unlike the fundamentalist and a bit like Socrates, knows that he does not know.) Strictly applied, this theology does not allow for the projection upon society of fantastic and strife-inducing spiritual visions of world affairs or utopian solutions. When such visions are unleashed upon us from religious sources, it is usually from sources which insist that their faith constitutes certain knowledge of God's will.

The rigors of Kierkegaardian faith make it a rare phenomenon; among the world's spiritual devotees, authentic Kierkegaardians are not much in evidence. The pervasive consideration—the one raising far-reaching questions about religion and moderation—is that monotheism imposes obligations of unconditional allegiance to the one God above all else, including our most cherished concerns and relationships.[52] And, as to the masses of believers, everything depends upon what their traditions and their leaders claim the Divinity has mandated. An important part of this question is *how much* of human life is deemed to be regulated by sacred requirements. When the mandates are deemed not only categorical but also totalitarian—that is, encompassing the entirety of personal and social life[53]—then the tension between religion and rational prudence is at its height.

Insofar as the tension we've been exploring threatens political moderation, three possible modes of alleviation come to mind. First, religious plurality—what James Madison called a "multiplicity of sects"—can alleviate by precluding the emergence of a monolithic zealotry. No need to elaborate this familiar point here, except to note that as such it doesn't preclude a multiplicity of fanatical sects. Second (and more controversially if stated bluntly), religious commitments could be softened, diluted (so to speak), or made less prominent in the lives of believers. This, I would argue, was one of the projects of that epoch-making philosophic movement called the Enlightenment, which sought to replace "superstition" with a rational and scientific view of reality. The project was meant to affect not only philosophic thought but also society at large and eventually the mind of the average person. Tocqueville, influenced in part by the Enlightenment, saw religion as an indispensable corrective for the self-centered materialism that democratic societies foster, but he was concerned about fanatical spirituality—"bizarre sects" and "religious follies" that drive their devotees "far beyond the bounds of common sense."[54] Evidently Tocqueville supposed that religious belief and practice should, and can, be tempered by common sense—that is, by a form of rationality.

This expectation seems at first glance quite implausible and at variance with things I've just said. But, after all, there are in the modern world many who are considered religious moderates, whose passion for the Eternal is either less fervent or more accommodating to the interests of secular society than was that of their ancestors. (Contemporary American Presbyterianism is a far cry from that of John Calvin and John Knox.) If this is what we mean by religious moderation, how can it come about on a large scale? You rarely bring it about by directly confronting true believers with rational arguments. It comes about largely because minds are affected gradually by the predominant social and ideological environment. Two elements of this process deserve special notice. Where science and technology flourish, where Enlightenment attitudes are "in the air," the effect is a kind of matter-of-fact mentality to which the mysterious and the mythological, including most aspects of scriptural revelation, are alien. Max Weber called this process "the disenchantment of the world." Another source of disenchantment is widespread taste for the numerous worldly gratifications and comforts that commercial modernity can confer. The bourgeois man is unlikely to become an inspired zealot, ideological or theological. (And, by the way, he is not the man to risk life for the sake of glory or "honor.") Hence, the dangers of fanaticism are alleviated.

This is an alleviation with difficulties of its own, including the danger that it will be carried far in the direction of spiritual indifference and a sophisticated disbelief that there can be anything mysterious or transcendent or more important than one's life, liberty, and property. We are therefore led to consider the third way of protecting the civic community from disruption by spiritually incited extremism. This antidote, usually called "separation of church and state," is one of the several defining features of a liberty polity, though it is not confined thereto. The idea most pertinent here is that when government is constitutionally prohibited from becoming an instrument for advancement of any religion, society is secured from one of the greatest threats to its harmony: the civil discord that results from struggles of religious groups for political power[55] and infection of political issues with sectarian or intolerant passions that make them uncompromisable. A legally mandated (or otherwise assured) distinction between legitimate concerns of state and religious concerns does not guarantee that either will be moderate, but it is a necessary condition for a politics reasonably prudential and balanced (consider the stark alternatives to this condition recently illustrated by Northern Ireland, Sudan, and Iran). Even extremism itself may eventually be tempered when zealots are compelled to face the fact that they cannot advance their cause through acquisition of governmental power.

But is an absolute separation of church and state a real possibility? Even where "an establishment of religion" is constitutionally prohibited, as by our First Amendment, the state and the church, the civic and the religious spheres, cannot be wholly insulated from each other. Multifarious occasions for their interaction exist, and where to draw the line is a never-ending perplexity confronting the federal courts. In principle, governmental policy crosses the line if it interferes with a religious practice because that practice is viewed as impious, deliberately favors some churches over others, or gives public funds directly to churches to be used for religious purposes. But what about the tax exemption for church properties, a "moment of silence" in public schools, the expression "under God" in the Pledge of Allegiance, the old practice of opening sessions of Congress and state legislatures with a chaplain's invocation, or the declaration of a day of Thanksgiving by the president of the United States?[56] Such traditions presuppose that recognition of the Deity has a place in American public life. That idea is what puristic separationists emphatically deny, some going so far as to seek the total exclusion of religious symbols and affirmations from the public sphere. This extremity of separationist fervor is itself a kind of absolutism; after all, we are devoted to "free exercise" as well as "no establishment," and religion does have a historic morality-promoting and ennobling role to play in this country. A jurisprudence of moderation on this subject will decide Establishment issues on a case-by-case basis, which allows for the recognition that there is more than one principle at stake and more than one good to be served or evil to be avoided. Hence even here there is such a thing as extremism and moderation. The latter recognizes the complex reality that in democracies faith-based morality is inevitably among the motivators of political causes or movements (sometimes desirably; sometimes not)—and that the utilization of government for objectives predominantly religious is the great danger to be avoided. This is no simple matter. On this subject, as on so many others concerning the public good, there is need for balanced judgment.

These brief references to legal matters point to a large topic without which our discussion would be incomplete: the idea of the rule of law. The law is often regarded as a great moderator, as is implied by the revered principle of "a government of laws not men."[57] In the tradition that invokes this idea, the law is seen as a body of general rules and principles standing above and regulating, more or less impartially, the unruly passions and biases of men. Insofar as this vision corresponds to reality, or can be made to do so, the need for statesmanship may be diminished.

This venerated idea is easy to ridicule. Here is what Thomas Hobbes, a relentless ridiculer, had to say:

> And therefore this is another error of Aristotle's politics, that in a well-ordered commonwealth, not men should govern but the laws. What man that has his natural senses, though he can neither write nor read, does not find himself governed by men he fears and believes can kill or hurt him when he obeyth not? Or believes the law can hurt him; that is, words and paper, without the hands and swords of men.[58]

To put it in less colorful language, laws are made and enforced by those persons or groups who have the power to do so; hence the law is not what actually *rules*—it cannot be the fundamental governor of a polity.

Aristotle recognized this reality. He indicated clearly enough that the laws inevitably reflect the wants and outlooks of those who make them, and that the constitution of a country is part and parcel of its political regime. (Oligarchic regimes will make laws on behalf of the property owners; democratic regimes will make egalitarian and redistributive ones on behalf of the many who are not economically well off, etc.)[59] Still, from the Aristotelian and classical perspectives, it makes a substantial difference how the governing interests are expressed—whether they are expressed as long-term general rules and principles or only as edicts and fiats dictated by the momentary will of either the few or the many. An oligarchy with a constitution is preferable to oligarchy raw and unrefined. A constitutional democracy is better than a wholly plebiscitary one.

As John Locke puts it, when you have "a standing rule to live by," enacted by the legislative authority, you are "not . . . subject to the inconsistent, uncertain, unknown, arbitrary will of another man."[60] By a "standing rule," Locke means one that has existed publicly for some length of time, and hence was enacted well in advance of the particular situations to which it is applied. Government by laws in this sense facilitates liberty by precluding certain arbitrary, unpredictable, coercive interventions in our lives. Where effective, such a legal order allows us to plan our lives in relatively secure awareness of what others will or won't do to us. (Motorists will usually stop at the red light, government officials will seldom break into your home without a warrant or probable cause, and taxes will be collected in accordance with some knowable standards or classifications.)

The rule of law, thusly understood, can also be viewed as a contributor to moderation. Laws deserving the name are results of deliberation about public interests much more comprehensive than the individual or factional interests to be regulated by them. Of course the legislative body is an arena for factional conflict and bargaining among self-interested or opinionated groups—hence the old joke about two things one doesn't want to see in the process of being produced: sausages and law. But with regard to the latter, the joke tells only half the story. When different viewpoints are in contention and contending arguments are made, the legislators are impelled to engage in some deliberation. And when a chosen policy is to have the authority of law, it must take the form of general rules applicable not only now but in a distant future and to persons one does not know. These requisites introduce an element of rationality operating within a horizon broader than that within which ordinary persons and groups in society usually operate. (The paradigmatic case is a constitutional convention.) This is the degree of truth embodied in the old and persistent idea that law is something dispassionate. Though bias and interest certainly enter into the production of law, the outcome—the rule intended to delimit conduct—is typically more dispassionate than you and I are in our everyday strivings and controversies. For example, the labor laws of the country might well be biased in favor of the workers or their employers, but they are much less so than the union and the corporation in the throes of a particular dispute.

But the virtue of law—its universality or generality—is sometimes a vice. The underlying reason for this anomaly, upon which I've already commented enough, is the variability and unruliness of human relations and problems that render them unamenable to dogmatic resolution or resolution simply by abstract precepts. We cannot, and wouldn't want to, be governed entirely by rules even if it were possible to construct thoroughly impartial ones. This reality mandates a large role for the prudential "judgment call," including—and especially—statesmanship. Even John Locke, who famously proclaimed that "no man in civil society can be exempted from the laws of it,"[61] finds it necessary to acknowledge the limits of the rule of law. "Many things there are which the law can by no means provide for, and those must necessarily be left to the discretion of him that has the executive power."[62] That is, there are many things that have to be decided outside the law and occasionally even against it. (As, arguably, Lincoln did when he authorized mass preventative detentions of Confederate supporters.) Matters of national security and foreign policy provide the foremost, but by no means the only, illustrations of that sometimes unpleasing reality.

Overemphasis upon the control of human affairs by general rules is what we are complaining about when we complain about "legalism," and legalism is also unpleasing, is it not? The rule of law is a blessing—where you can really have it—but, like separation of church and state, it is a moderator itself in need of modification.

I cannot leave this subject, however, without tribute to the aspiration for impartiality or disinterestedness that is at the heart of the idea of the rule of law. The ideal model is the image we have of the judge scrupulously weighing both sides of the case in the scales of justice and with a view to the truth. As far as civic life is concerned, this is the concept of moderation at its pinnacle.[63] Moderation at this judicial height—the capacity to distance oneself from partisan claims and even from one's own inclinations—is a rare thing; it hardly comes naturally. Where we can get approximation to it, in courts and elsewhere, the approximations usually depend much upon institutional and public support for the enterprise, that is, a public opinion that respects and believes in it. And such a public opinion will depend upon a delicate combination of education and inspiration to counteract our natural partisanship.

Liberal education, at its best, promotes respect for impartiality by placing us at a certain intellectual distance from immediacy, facilitating a disposition to stand back from the ideological clamor of our time and reflect upon ideas "on all sides" of questions perennial. It encourages what may be called a theoretical perspective or a contemplative one. The emphasis upon theory and alternative theories characteristic of a good liberal education can perform a distancing function for those citizens amenable to it. The philosophic model here is Socratic truth-seeking, which seeks understanding for its own sake.[64]

This has been an effort to identify the several dimensions of political moderation and to show how, despite its vicissitudes, this concept is broadly appropriate in the complex affairs of such beings as we are. Moderation, as we've seen, is not so much a particular policy as it is an attitude, a disposition, an orientation. The orientation defined here is not the only political virtue, nor is it always the most important thing, but it is always important. This orientation is possible because we are self-conscious beings with the potentiality for reflective detachment, occasionally even from ourselves. It is needed because our reflections, more often than not, become the instruments of passion—loves and hates, anger and compassion, fears and hopes (frequently excessive), and pride, which can take the form of vanity or lust for power. We are much concerned with self-centered material gratifications but able to aspire beyond material interests to more spiritual ones, with results sometimes elevating, sometimes quite harmful. Exaggerated hopes for a better social life may lead us to entertain unrealistically absolute solutions and long for (dangerous) utopias. Maximalist demands upon the world, conjoined with anger, are at the core of much fanaticism and strife. So too are fervent beliefs, fueled by human pride, that the great tensions and uncertainties of life are intolerable and can be eradicated by application of pure rationality. We are such beings as can be led astray by excessive claims or pretenses to knowledge as well as by irrational appetites and emotions.

Most simply put, the case for political moderation rests finally on the realization that human nature is located as far from the purely benign as it is from the simply bestial, and our various inclinations are often in contradiction. Moderation then is not only a necessary virtue: it is also a fragile virtue.

Chapter 2

Personal Moderation
Taming the Excess

The primary purpose of the aforegoing essay was to articulate a definition of moderation, especially as related to public affairs. As a definition
it presents only an outline of the subject and its key elements: balance
or proportionality, recognition of limits, some capacity for disinterestedness—and the type of character that sustains them. The secondary
purpose was to show why you should want a politics incorporating these
qualities, and why you should be quite afraid of any leaders, movements,
or polities wholly lacking them.

Perhaps it is not so difficult to show that we'd better have these moderating qualities, and, to paraphrase a great poet, the center ought to
hold, in the political side of life. But what about the private side of life and
those aspects of our existence that transcend or precede public affairs?
The observations about moral character, and about reason and passion,
upon which (with qualifications) my argument has largely relied, are
hardly complex enough to provide a sufficient basis for conclusions about
requisites of a successful personal life or a healthy one.

It could be that what moderation means and requires in public affairs
is not the same thing as what it means and requires for the individual and
interpersonal relations; perhaps there is even a divergence between the

two desiderata. More radically, modern viewpoints, needing some attention, dismiss the very idea of moderation as a key either to our understanding of the human condition or our flourishing in it; they envision rather different keys. Couldn't one say that flourishing, at bottom, has nothing to do with any rational balancing but is a matter of vitality—living energetically and spontaneously? Or of audacity—a spirited willingness to take large risks? Or of love, which is inevitably unbalanced? If sheer vigor or audacity or love is what it is all about—if these are the main routes to happiness, or if one of them is its crucial component—then there is apparently little to be said on behalf of mere moderation and the personality type associated with it. Of course, these are questions of what is good for us. But then what of the radical philosophic claim that all such questions are unanswerable, being entirely dependent upon subjective moral opinions, indemonstrable assumptions about human nature, and ideological constructs that purport to give us unbiased representations of reality but cannot do so? We are forced to consider whether, and in what way, there may be a center that can hold under such challenges.

To begin at the surface, there is a type of easygoing, self-satisfied equanimity that sometimes passes as moderation. This personality lives largely if not entirely with a view to material security, comfort, and a continuing supply of modest gratifications; his predominant effort is focused upon the acquisition of the material instruments conducive thereto. He demands little but thinks well of himself, devotes much attention to physical health or longevity, and engages in activities as harmless to others as to himself. The emergence into prominence of this figure in what is termed bourgeois society is a subject much observed and commented upon in literature from the eighteenth century to the present. In its current incarnation this mode of life is infused with large doses of an egalitarian moral relativism; one refuses to make any judgments about alternative lifestyles, thereby avoiding offense and any need to justify one's own. If there is a moral imperative here it is: "Thou shalt not be judgmental." (In the crude vernacular, "I'm OK; you're OK, equally.")

Nietzsche, a profound diagnostician of modern tendencies, was not in a position to observe empirically this latest incarnation, but he forcefully predicted it. Of the personalities he envisioned modernity would produce, Nietzsche writes, "They have their little pleasures for the day, and their little pleasures for the night, but they have a regard for health."[1] On account of the pettiness of their interests and smallness of their vision, Nietzsche, who did not eschew judgmentalism, called them "the last men"—those who "maketh everything small."[2]

Whether or not you agree with the harshness of that evaluation, do you want to regard the type of person under consideration as an exemplar of moderation? Yes, you might say; he is, as the expression goes, "at home in his own skin," and, lacking irregular passion, he is no threat to his neighbors, and he obeys the law because lawfulness is conducive to security and prosperity. Or no, one might answer; his equanimity has not been won through any struggle or even effort; it is the result of obliviousness to the heights and depths of existence. He never thinks of wrestling, as the statesman periodically does, with weighty conflicts among the diverse goods, principles, and possibilities that human affairs can present; he has faced neither temptation nor anomalies. Lacking strong desires or large aspirations, he has little need for the cultivation of self-control or the enterprise of balancing. That is, he has little occasion for cultivating those qualities and capabilities that define moderation, because he never encounters the realities that make it a virtue important to possess. Isn't it better to call a condition like that utmost "mediocrity," and to regard it not as a middle ground but as an extreme case among the alternative ways of being?

Philosophic and literary indictments of mediocrity often fail to make the distinction I'm suggesting; the indictments become attacks on moderation as such. When this is done it is usually on behalf of passion or vitality. Hence Nietzsche condemns those moral orientations which function as recipes against the dangerousness of our passions, including "the tuning down of the affects to a harmless mean according to which they may be satisfied: the Aristotlelianism of morals."[3]

Now there is a current outlook among us whose distaste for moralities of temperance and self-control rests on the assumption that the emotions sought to be controlled are by nature benign and undangerous; hostilities and aggressions arise, it is said, only when these affects are suppressed by externally imposed restraints. Thus, an ethic of restraint is denigrated in favor of an ethic of self-expression, which is definitely un-Nietzschean. Nietzsche recognized (indeed famously asserted) the existence of elemental human urges that are far from benign, and, in contrast with some of his admirers, he envisioned a significant role for discipline—various intellectual, moral, and spiritual disciplines that, historically, have inculcated "value," that is, provided grounds for aspiration. But the disciplinary constraints he recognized as contributors to human development are hardly derived from reasoning; their origins are deeply irrational.[4]

Is there, after all, a place for moderation even in Nietzschean philosophy? Insofar as there is, it is most manifest in the distinction he makes between "the Apollonian" and "the Dionysian" in an early work, *The Birth of Tragedy*. Here is an interpretive simplification. Apollo is the deity of order, harmony, and enlightenment; Dionysius is the deity of the Bacchanalian orgy and frenzied passion. The former stands for a worldview featuring "that measured restraint, that freedom from the wilder emotions, that philosophic calm," according to which excess and pride are viewed as vices.[5] The latter glories in impulsive excess, finds joy in the transcendence of all venerable boundaries, and liberates "savage natural instincts," including "that horrible mixture of sensuality and cruelty."[6] Now, as I read it, the latter impulses are natural; we are told that "the basis of all existence is the Dionysian substratum of the world."[7] On the other hand, the Apollonian is a product of art, which creates comforting and inspiring representations of reality that make it possible for us to live purposefully on earth despite the horrible substratum. These representations aim to supplant our perceptions of the terrifying and the absurd with life-supporting myths; that is to say, healthy illusions.

Now on this account of things, why should one denigrate the Aristotelianism of morals? Why not regard "nothing in excess," and the worldview from which it arises, as one of those salutary Apollonian illusions serving to order our lives meaningfully despite the Dionysian realities? The falsity of that outlook is hardly an argument against it upon which Nietzsche could rely. An argument he could advance more con-sistently is that the trouble with the Aristotelianism of morals is not its untruth but that (especially under degenerative modern conditions) it devitalitizes. Why? It puts reason in the driver's seat—an abstract, blood-less form of cognition and calculation that has never gazed into the abyss of Dionysian chaos. Contrary to such bloodless reasoning, a genuinely Apollonian vision is a reaction to our intuition of the terrible forces that have to be overcome; it is never wholly out of contact with those forces. Indeed it can be said to derive its energy from their energy; perhaps the term "sublimation" is appropriate here.[8] At any rate, the Apollonian is dependent upon the Dionysian, and vitality—more accurately, creative vitality—depends upon their interaction. Nietzsche has to denigrate moderation insofar as its rational balancing, recognition of limits, and efforts at disinterestedness are disconnected from the emotive power he sees at the base of existence.

Yet a reader of Nietzsche may perceive that moderation is not wholly denigrated in all of its forms; it has the status of an ambiguity. Nietzsche recognizes our need for "limits," though the limits are man-made and impermanent. The various moral and spiritual disciplines (and aes-thetic ones; Nietzsche celebrates great music) that, historically, we have imposed upon the chaos of our affective drives perform a salutary func-tion in the refinement and ordering of raw impulse, though the refine-ments and orderings are rooted in the irrational. Moderation of a sort thus plays a role as contributor to human flourishing—a secondary and derivative role. But when severed from the passionate sources of inspi-ration, as nowadays it always is, the Aristotelianism of morals can only result in a toning down of the affects to a harmless, apathetic mean that prepares the way for "the last man." This disaster is finally attributed both to rationalism and fear; we are afraid of any vigorous impulses that could disturb tranquility and threaten our comfortable security.

Let us begin a rebuttal with the observation that it would be strange to depict Aristotelian ethics per se as a philosophy dominated by a secu-rity-minded timidity. As I've noted, courage is a prominent Aristotelian vÍrtue, and by definition it means that the personality governed by fear is defective at least as much as the reckless one. The man extolled as courageous is, under appropriate conditions, willing to risk his life. And, be it further noted, the asserted aim of all the virtues is not personal safety but capability (one of the root meanings of *arête*, the Greek word usually translated as virtue), the capability or strength to act in confrontation with life's recurrent challenges. Regarding the supposedly enervating rationalism of classical moderation, it is important to have clearly in mind (as Nietzsche apparently did not) the critical Aristotelian distinction between theoretical and practical wisdom. According to that distinction, abstract knowledge or theory is not what guides us toward the mean between extremes; what guides us is a practical and experiential insight about variable particular situations and their bearing upon our overall well-being. This prudential enlightenment or, as we may call it, worldly wisdom is a kind of reasoning, but it is by no means bloodless. (Here, it seems to me, is a compelling illustration of the point: consistently insightful judgment about the character of persons you deal with must be a significant component of worldly wisdom, and such an understanding of other people has to involve a combination of cognition, experience, and feeling, doesn't it?) Far from presiding tyrannically over our affects, wisdom, as Aristotle tells us, can only exist in intimate connection with "right desire," for one's desires affect one's perception of reality—for better or worse.[9] Now right desires are said to depend usually upon virtuous habits that make up good character; untutored, therefore excessive, passions will distort perceptions of reality. Character, and this tutoring or tempering function of it, is another of those classical concepts that Nietzsche largely neglects. Finally let us observe that the "last man" is enervated because his way of life is an easy and complacent one; he undertakes nothing difficult. Aristotle writes, "In everything it is no easy task to find the middle. . . . Therefore goodness is both rare and laudable and noble."[10]

Would Nietzsche soften his critique if he had to acknowledge the import of moral character and of practical wisdom, as agencies distinct from the abstract conceptualization and calculation of which he was so suspicious? My guess is that even then he would deny that these things are fundamental; classical moderation would have to be downgraded because it refuses to recognize the primacy of the Dionysian. Moreover the ideal fruition of moderation in the classical tradition is a kind of unity in the soul, harmony among the diverse elements naturally inhabiting the psyche; ultimately wholeness is what balance is about.[11] Nietzsche contradicts that ideal; in this speech to the predecessors of "the last man," he has his Zarathustra proclaim: "I tell you: one must still have chaos in one to give birth to a dancing star. I tell you: ye still have chaos in you."[12]

This question of concord and discord in the soul or the psyche or the self is central to our topic. The ancients and the Nietzscheans agree, more or less, on one thing: inner concord is not our natural or spontaneous condition; we are naturally divided beings whose different components are at least potentially in conflict. But for the ancients, harmony, however difficult to achieve, is the desideratum; Nietzsche critically diverges from this traditional picture of the final desideratum.

Nietzsche welcomes the presence of inner chaos, that is, a warfare of irreconcilable drives, as the condition and stimulus of creative vitality— which is what really counts. Only on such a basis can superior human beings arise whose task it is to "create new values."[13] These are men who can muster from the psychic depths what Nietzsche's later work calls "the will to power," a spirited will to mastery—the mastery not only of external things and people but also of one's divided self. It draws upon an elementary instinct, but its highest function is the genesis of radically new orders of meaning and evaluation of what is "good" for us to be imposed upon self and others. Thus are ordered forms constructed and projected upon formless reality by endless exercises of creative volition that are not launched fundamentally for the sake of order but fundamentally for the sake of mastery.

Underlying Nietzsche's account of the will to power at its creative pinnacle is a vision of what constitutes healthy and unhealthy existence; a vigorously self-assertive will is the requisite and sign of health. And it is in the nature of such a will that it is a relentless struggle to predominate—to overcome contrary forces internal as well as external. In this endeavor turbulence is not to be avoided or eradicated or denigrated; turbulence is welcomed as a necessary challenge and an inspiration. Nietzsche juxtaposes his model of life—a version of the "heroic" model—against that of the comfort-seeking equanimity engendered, as he sees it, by rationalist and egalitarian modernity. But there is another sort of equanimity, which is the one classically recommended as the optimal condition: you have encountered the contrary forces in the soul and your understanding of them allows for their arrangement in a kind of friendly accord whereby your various natural powers, when fully developed or refined, will support each other. Out of the many in the soul there arises a oneness, and this harmony is good health. On such a basis a person can accept, with a measure of composure, the stubborn reality that there are conflicts and evils in the world over which he will not be able to triumph but to which, with the requisite inner composure, he can apply prudence and practical moral judgment. At any rate, we have to conclude that the Nietzchean archetype of a worthy life is that of ceaseless struggle and agitation wherein the will to power is never at rest; here moderation and the cognition associated with it are remote from the driver's seat.

One reason I have devoted so much attention to Nietzsche is that he casts a long shadow, an influence extending even to some who would recoil from his fundamentals if they understood them. Prominent among our intelligentsia are moral liberationists or postmodernists who celebrate impulse over rationality and creativity over truth-seeking. Yet not many are so intemperate as to accord "savage natural instincts" and a "mixture of sensuality and cruelty" the status that Nietzsche gave them. (Writers like Norman Mailer and literati impressed with the Marquis de Sade come to mind as exceptions.) But, among those of our contemporaries who remain disposed to render judgments about the worthy and the unworthy, there are many whose touchstones for evaluation are, implicitly or explicitly, vitalistic, and who seem bent upon teaching us to despise more than anything the uncreative middle-class man.

More than anything? My uncle was such a middle-class man. He never once invented a value or looked into the chaotic abyss; he accepted the norms he inherited (some of religious origin), kept his passions under control, took care of his family, and practiced the ordinary decencies. It would be unfair to think of him as a "last man," though he was hardly an exciting man. The Marquis de Sade was a much more intense personality; perhaps you would find de Sade's company more interesting than that of my uncle, for a time anyway. But if you had to choose for the long run which of these two personality types is the preferable neighbor, companion, or fellow citizen, would you have any serious doubt? My point here is not that my uncle is the model of a moderate man; the point is about us as evaluators. Few of us are so enamored of sheer energy that, confronted with such a choice, we would opt for the Marquis. Would Nietzsche? One is hard put to envision why not.

The Nietzschean themes usually reach us in somewhat softened versions. In a poem entitled "Vitality," D. H. Lawrence proclaims:

> You might as well take the lightning
> for once and feel it go through you.
> You might as well accept the thunderbolt
> and prepare for the storms.
> You'll not get vitality any other way.[14]

As poet, Lawrence is under no obligation to spell out what he means by the lightning and the thunderbolt; from his major writings we can infer that he probably does not mean to include savage cruelties. But these writings tell us that to be really alive you must give yourself to a grand passion and boldly run the risks of going where it leads. Being fully alive is what really matters, and the requisite for that, as Lawrence indicates elsewhere, is that you find and audaciously follow your own "demon."

This rather romantic view of human fulfillment can be attractive. On its face, it doesn't require that you exercise a severe will to power or wrestle perpetually with contradictory and terrible impulses of the psyche. Nietzsche would be unsatisfied with it; no doubt he would agree with Lawrence that the unenergetic life is not worth living, but he would find the romantic outlook optimistically deficient regarding the underlying sources of the authentically energetic. Paradoxically, insofar as Romanticism ignores or slights the dangerously Dionysian, it provides less room for a moderating self-discipline than Nietzsche does. Lawrence might reply, along with many of us, that Nietzsche has made more of the darkest side of Dionysius than is warranted. Let us suppose, for the sake of argument, that what exists at the bottom of the soul is a life force or élan vital, and if you can muster the courage to liberate it from obstructions of largely social construction, it can flourish as grand passion.

Moderation would then be seen as one of the big obstructions. Grand passion, if one is serious about it, means wholehearted devotion to something or someone—a devotion overriding all else and activated by what Lawrence calls one's "demon." This has nothing to do with any weighing and balancing of competing goods, imperatives, or obligations; indeed, balancing is incompatible with such passion, the hallmark of which is no compromise. Furthermore, you are much indisposed to recognize limits, or you will strive to surpass or push back any limits encountered. Moreover, your mentality is the opposite of disinterestedness; in other words, nowhere in your consciousness is there an element standing back, critically distanced from your passion and its object.[15]

In light of this vision, moderation appears as a pale and paltry thing. You have only one life; do you really want to spend it in a series of petty accommodations or in the service of affects enervated by reservations? The proponent of moderation could offer these (perhaps unexciting) responses: You have fallen into a sizable error about the human condition; your basic mistake is to ground everything in some underlying élan vital, universal or personal. Actually we are reasoning and social beings as well as emotive ones, and so "living to the fullest" must include the fulfillment of our capacities for thought and for sociality. Can we really credit as an energetic human life one in which these faculties are undeveloped and unenergized? This is the initial argument to be made against the irrationalist. A second line of argument is that, as complex social beings, we are rarely without diverse imperatives requiring consideration; various claims upon us include those of family, friends, career, and community, as well as one's own good, not just for now but for the long run. Is it your idea that all such claims should be sacrificed to one great desire? If not, then you have to make room for some weighing and balancing superintended by thought. What if the demands of a promising career would require neglect of your family? What if loyalty to friends is at variance with loyalty to country (suppose your closest friend decides to become a supporter of al-Qaida)? How much do I owe and to whom and to what?

An existentialist answer to such dilemmas is, there being no rational ethical guidelines, one can only resolve them by making a decisive choice, arbitrary though it might be. Whatever we may think of the existentialist solution, it provides no aid and comfort to the Romanticist, for it will not allow one to rely upon an answer dictated by a preexisting passion or a personal "demon." For the Sartrean existentialist anyway, what's crucial is personal autonomy; I define, indeed create, myself by decisions having no basis either in passions or reason. Sartre's man defines himself by inventing his own values "alone, unjustified and without excuse," and thus he takes full responsibility for them. You are not taking responsibility if you tell yourself "a passion made me do it"; such a ploy is self-deceptive, and self-deception (*mauvois fois*) is the worst thing, indeed the only truly bad thing, in a world where standards of value are all groundless. Hence, you are perfectly free to choose friends over country or country over friends, and anything else, so long as you are making an authentically self-conscious choice.[16] This view has as little use for moderation as does the romantic one; believing that you are obliged to temper your choices would be another, and perhaps especially egregious, form of self-deception.

The question necessarily arises of what kind of responsible agent you can be where there are no guidelines whatever (except those you arbitrarily invent) for judging to what or whom one ought to be responsible. The philosophy of moderation has a place for autonomy, though (if I may say so) a more modest place, as a good to be considered among others; of course, there must be moral space for my exercise of free agency, even eccentrically, but how much space when other goods might be damaged? The reflective moderate knows that such questions have to be faced without the pretense that they are resolvable by a self-creating act of will or by a great and overriding impulse.

The principle of autonomy, while dubious in its absolute form, can serve to provide moderation with a further argument. The grand passion of the Lawrentian hero, like that of the glory-seeking hero, would seem to be all-consuming; what happens to freedom of choice under such an impulsion? After all, dedicated Romantics are not speaking of tamed or gentrified appetites—quite the contrary. A real freedom of choice apparently requires that, however pressing one's passion might be, there remains in the consciousness some agency unconsumed by it, therefore in a position to make a determination about it. And that agency is hard to conceive as something apart from reason. Here we see quite a problem for those intent upon regarding enthronement of the irrational as liberation.

Yet these arguments seem insufficient. Perhaps when our subject is well-being in the personal, as distinguished from the public or political, side of life, there is more to be said on behalf of the emotive and on behalf of audacity. As to audacious risk-taking, think of climbers of Mount Everest, bungee jumpers, and various daredevils who enthusiastically embrace dangers. Do we want to dismiss altogether as immoderation the exhilaration they seek? It is obvious why we would blame political leaders who pursued the dangerous for its own sake and for the excitement of it. But private individuals who do that are often admired as adventurous—within limits (we don't admire the habitual gambler, and Russian roulette or its equivalents are considered deranged). What are the adventurers after? Fame for daring the extraordinary? The experience of an intensified spiritedness? As for our admiration, it might be interpreted as a need to take holidays from moderation; alternatively, the way we conceptualize what moderation means might need some adjustment to accommodate occasions of wild enthusiasm. A similar point can be made about other irrational inclinations; sometimes one should express and act upon them—sometimes zest for living depends upon allowing latitude for the excessive. To loosely paraphrase Pascal, "It is not reasonable to be always rational; reason had better listen to the emotions." This much should be conceded by a sensibly adjusted understanding of moderation; for such complex beings as we are, a balanced life, or equilibrium in a soul that includes spirited impulses, is no simple enterprise. But, according to the adjusted understanding, it is one thing to enjoy occasions of wildness and quite another to be a wild person—always out of control or driven over long stretches of time by insatiable urges (like figures Dostoevsky so powerfully portrays). Here character appears as a critical factor; controls can be relaxed desirably insofar as you have a moral constitution habitually or normally self-controlling, and the demands of rationality may be relaxed by a mind in which reason retains a prominent voice.

At this point romantics, and not only certified Romantics, may protest that all of this ignores love, which is a passion central to the happiness of almost everyone. And love does not calculate.

Many of us regard erotic love as the most vitalizing experience on earth. Some say that under its spell the whole world becomes beautiful and inviting; that this is an illusion—who cares? Others say that when you are in the powerful grip of this experience the whole world disappears; who cares what Congress or the Supreme Court are doing about public interests?

What do we mean by "love"? Here, in a poem called "The Extasie," is what John Donne meant:

> When love with one another so
> Interanimates two soules,
> That abler soule, which hence doth flow,
> Defects of loneliness ountroules.[17]

In the impoverished language of our contemporary sexology, the poem would be seen as a depiction of two people "having sex." But for Donne this is love because it is about the intimate uniting of "two soules," and it is sex because that fruition cannot occur without union of the bodies; that, primarily, is why "we [lovers] to our bodies turn." It should be noted that the poem as a whole presupposes the distinction between body and psyche—a distinction regarded by numerous psychologists and physiologists (and by Nietzsche) as thoroughly discredited. Ordinary experience apparently sides with Donne. Ordinarily one is aware of a "self" that is not simply one's body; after all, it is *my* body, belonging to *me*. Though the erotic is always mysterious enough to preclude any complete objective understanding of it, what seems to happen at its culmination is that the differentiation of body and psyche we usually experience is overcome by an experience of their union.[18] The intense passion associated with this intimate joining together is, in Donne's terminology, ecstatic. But equally important in this account of the matter is that love powerfully merges the identities of two persons who are deficient when alone, or as separate identities; it is an affectionate communion overcoming the isolation of our individuality.

In this scene, moderation is hard to find. The erotic encounter per se has little, if any, room for self-control; especially at or near its consummation, what is called for is surrender—a surrender of control and even of self as the boundaries between lovers dissolves. This is one of the reasons why sexual love is so often said to be a "delicate" matter and persons engaged in it "vulnerable." It would appear that one's ability to accept this condition of vulnerability is a prerequisite for loving, and a stubborn insistence upon retaining one's self-possession in such situations is at least counterproductive and may be considered a disability.

Shall we acknowledge then that in this crucial area of life moderation is out of place, even pathological? This is rough ground for a candid proponent of it, who, I believe, has to respond with a yes and a no. Who can deny that in the intensity of sexual encounters one is not reasoning, and self-command is eclipsed? Any systematic effort to have it otherwise would lend itself to ridicule as unnatural and provide inviting subject matter for comedy (a temperate ecstasy?) And, it will be argued, the exclusion of moderation from this domain amounts to a considerable demotion of its status as contributor to our well-being.

This argument is successful insofar as it persuades us to view all the phases of erotic love from the perspective of its final and physical consummation. But what about "falling in love"? Shall we concede that reasoning, self-command, and character can have no role in determining with whom one falls (and remains) in love? There is a kind of conventional wisdom which pronounces that you just can't help it. Of course, one does not deliberately choose to be in love as one may deliberately decide upon a career or a political party. However, it is a considerable leap from that conclusion to the conclusion that, with regard to this whole subject, judgment, and hence choice, are irrelevant or without effect. If you don't want happiness and unhappiness to be a kind of lottery, you had better be in some position to judge the qualities of the person you consider giving yourself to and cherishing. If love is a passionate identification with another, you don't want to identify with someone so dishonest, manipulative, or self-centered as to be incapable of mutuality. (Much of what goes on in Jane Austen's novels is the heroine's searching reflection about the qualities of the man in whom she might be interested. Who is he really? Is he trustworthy? Is he worthy of my devotion?)

I am making three intertwined points. First, even if the inquiry is confined to romantic love, we can't avoid recognizing the import of character. Second, even regarding romance, a thoroughgoing nonjudgmentalism wouldn't be good for you. Third, even here, where passion is so prominent, there is a place for the faculty of choosing.

In the present context the terms "character" and "moderation" are almost interchangeable, as the latter provides the basis for the former. A prime condition of good character, as ordinarily understood, is that you can say no to an impulse; you are able to resist the immediate demands of desire or pleasure at least long enough to allow for thinking about what should be done or avoided. There is (as is manifest in this inquiry) much more to it, but everything else depends upon this more or less habitual capacity for self-restraint.

I have formulated the proposition this way with the following counterargument in mind. Self-discipline is not in itself a good thing; it is a morally neutral capacity, which, after all, can be employed in the service of purposes good or ill. The 9/11 terrorists had to be very self-controlling and able to defer gratifications. There are two answers. The ability to say no to impulses is a necessary condition for an ensemble of characteristics (noted as the text proceeds) that are normally requisites of flourishing. And while the 9/11 terrorists were extraordinarily self-controlling with regard to ordinary human passions, they were not so with regard to those fundamental in their case—their virulent hatreds and religiosity. A characteristic is unwisely labeled as merely neutral in a moral sense if its presence is usually conducive to the beneficent and its absence is usually deleterious.

The connection between character and love may be depicted in various ways. You want your lover to be reliable, and a thoroughly immoderate individual is thoroughly unreliable. (The same goes, by the way, for friendship.) Moreover, the question arises whether a person very deficient in the capacity to resist impulse—sensual or other—is really capable of love. Love (in the substantial and not simply metaphorical sense) means that you are concerned about the other person for his or her own sake, and the relationship therefore is much more than an instrument of one's own gratifications. If this is to be a lasting union—as true lovers intend—frustrations, small and large, are inevitably encountered and major compromises of self-interest often required, and for meeting these demands or vicissitudes Eros alone is notoriously insufficient. Perhaps I am stating the obvious, but these things are not so obvious in all attitudes toward the subject or in all commentaries about it.[19]

Here is a consideration implicit in what I've been saying but warranting explication: some "loves" are disastrous. W. Somerset Maugham's novel *Of Human Bondage* graphically portrays a protagonist hopelessly and helplessly infatuated with a young woman who doesn't care about him and hardly seems an appropriate recipient of all that affection. But the protagonist cannot let go; his love is a perpetual enslavement. He would have been far better off exercising some judgmental choice before the emotion overwhelmed him. Psychiatric thought might suggest that this is not love; it is a pathological dependency. The implication is that radical dependency reflects a personality weakness; one has insufficient ego strength or self-esteem or ability to rely upon self-definition; hence he is in desperate need of someone else to define him. (In Nietzschean terms, this condition is the opposite of a healthy will to power.) But we encounter a perplexity here; love *is* a kind of dependency, isn't it? According to viewpoints like John Donne's, the individual, or the "self," is incomplete and in need of that intimate union with another in order to achieve completion. And according to almost everyone's view, loving entails vulnerability, a not altogether safe enterprise. But whether one thinks of the "human bondage" phenomenon as a pathological dependency or as a vicissitude of love, the general conclusion following is that you had better bring to the enterprise some substantial inner resources of your own. In other words, as is periodically noted, love is not enough.

Freud, unsurprisingly, had something to say about this problem. Freud's psychoanalytic account of our subject is not very romantic. In his *Civilization and Its Discontents*, love is treated as one of several possible "techniques of living" by which the individual strives for happiness, that is, more pleasure than pain, in a world full of formidable obstacles to pleasure and occasions for suffering. Among the various alternative strategies of pleasure-seeking and pain avoidance, there is "the way of life which makes love the center of everything, which looks for all satisfaction in loving and being loved. A psychical attitude of this sort comes naturally enough to all of us; one of the forms in which love manifests itself—sexual love—has given us our most intense experience of an overwhelming sensation of pleasure."[20] Love is such a popular aspiration among us because it allows for the gratification of a primal instinct—both directly and (where there is a lasting bond) in the modified or "sublimated" form that involves affection. Why not settle for this as the best practical resolution of the problem of happiness? "The weak side of this technique of living is easy to see . . . It is that we are never so defenseless against suffering as when we love, never so hopelessly unhappy as when we have lost our love object or its love."[21] The enterprise of loving, while it may promise the greatest fulfillment—when you can maintain it—also threatens the greatest unfulfillment when you cannot. It is interesting that Freud follows these reflections with what looks like a general injunction to moderation. "Any choice that is pushed to an extreme will be penalized by exposing the individual to the dangers which arise if a technique of living that has been chosen as an exclusive one should prove inadequate. Just as a cautious business-man avoids tying up all his capital in one concern, so, perhaps, worldly wisdom will advise us not to look for the whole of our satisfaction from a single aspiration."[22]

A reader of that passage should pay attention to its "perhaps"; this is Freud offering worldly or practical wisdom and not a rigorous conclusion of psychoanalytic theory. Freud's analysis of the human condition has raised critical questions. How far can this concept of pleasure and pain go in accounting for what human striving is about, especially when the former is understood essentially in terms of instinctual gratification? Lovers rarely view themselves as deploying a technique whereby primal lusts are most effectively enjoyed when sufficiently redirected (via mechanisms like sublimation) so as to facilitate a pleasurable bond. Ordinarily those who care the most about loving—whether as practi-tioners or as commentators—are much inclined to regard it as a primary need of our nature, and not as a secondary, derivative, or instrumental one. And we are inclined to think that sensual pleasure is only part of the story, perhaps even a derivative part. Freudian psychoanalysis would tend to view such attitudes suspiciously; ordinary perceptions of life are held to be unreliable, infected as they are by mental distortions or illusions through which the psyche seeks to make reality more attractive than it is. On this point—the prominence of the illusory in what we regard as common sense—as on other things, the Freudian outlook reminds us of Nietzsche's outlook.

Yet Freud gives the impression that he is at least somewhat serious about the validity of worldly wisdom—that which counsels us against, as the saying goes, putting all your eggs in one basket. In language less vulgar and more psychoanalytic, you should try to distribute your libido, or psychic energy, among a variety of objects, as the business person distributes capital, so as to avoid the danger of losing everything. Let us leave aside the issue of whether, in light of Freud's rather deterministic theory of human motivation, especially the prominence he accords to unconscious motivation, anyone has a real choice about how to live. Assuming some degree of choice, do we want a life conducted on the model of the cautious investor? No, a Nietzschean would say; this is a contemptible security-mindedness, like that of the "last man" who has his "little pleasures for the day . . . little pleasures for the night," all confined by "a regard for health." And devotees of love often insist that it is an exclusive passion taking precedence over all else, or it is not love.

Though I wouldn't have the question answered with a simple yes, there is much to be said for Freud's practical wisdom. It is almost self-evident that you are not only safer but also in better emotional health when seeking satisfaction through several aspirations, kept in some balance, than entirely through one. A single object of desire—be it love, family, career, politics, or even self-sufficiency—that is unbalanced by anything else can easily become a narrow fixation resembling addiction.[23] As for love, it has more substance when the persons engaged have more to bring to it; arguably it is not love when that is all you have.

Achievement of psychic health, in one of its dimensions, may be seen as a problem concerning the diversification or the concentration of energies. Freud's practical suggestion is that you ought to diversify as best you can. The opposite view is that, if you want to amount to anything, you had better concentrate your energies upon a cherished goal. Needless to say, this perennial dilemma cannot be resolved for everyone by any theory; speculation upon it, however, is too tempting to avoid. How does the concept of moderation apply to this question? It would appear that the concept comes down squarely on the side of diversity; moderation is associated with recognition that there is always a plurality of goods to be sought or legitimate considerations tugging in different directions, and the grand passion romantics extol is to be judged, on account of its one-sidedness, as unhealthy extremism. But couldn't we say that diversification can also be carried to an extreme, especially when its result is that one's libido is dispersed and scattered among a wide variety of small (and most likely tentative) interests? Where is the focus of such a life, and what is one's identity?[24]

While Freud's model of the cautious investor has its use, a different model might be more helpful: liberal education. An often asserted proposition is that a liberal education broadens one's horizons via the experience of intellectual diversity; the variety of the subjects studied and perspectives encountered is envisioned as the prime educator. Yet in any serious curriculum the student is required to have a major, to concentrate upon a subject, immersing him or herself in something and learning it (we hope) rather well. There is a balance to be struck between these two desiderata of education—breadth and depth—because each can be overemphasized at the expense of the other. While we do not have recourse to any universal rule that would specify the correct equilibrium (hence the recurrent curricular debates), we can recognize the evils to be avoided: superficiality on the one side and overspecialization on the other.

To be sure, it is rather more difficult to arrange a well-balanced life than a well-balanced college curriculum, but the analogy is appropriate enough to allow for the observation that, in the distribution of one's energies, there is such a thing as too much dispersal and too much specialization. The former condition makes for a superficial personality, which may be considered undesirable not so much on account of pleasure and pain as on account of purpose and purposelessness; do you want to skate over the surface of life without digging in, without finding something you care deeply about and concentrating upon it? The latter condition, a kind of emotionally overspecialized personality, may be considered undesirable on account of the narrow range of its interests and very limited horizons and consequently the impairment of its capacity for self-examination. Insofar as seriousness of purpose is at issue, a Socratic perspective would suggest that this is not well served by narrowness of horizons; how serious really is a purpose that is never examined? Indispensable for self-examination, apparently, is a capacity for reflective psychological distance from the demands of an ambition or a longing, and that usually depends upon an awareness of, or some openness to, alternatives.[25] Our education model suggests a possibility of avoiding entrapment in either of the extremities threatened by the dilemma of diversity and concentration. You may, so to speak, "major" in one aspect of life, focusing upon it while maintaining other significant interests and responsibilities; this is a posture that the concept of moderation can recommend. You will say that this generality is unhelpful; tensions will exist between one's primary and one's secondary devotions, and at critical junctures of events either compromise or painful sacrifices will have to be made. Such tensions are unavoidable by any general orientation that could be recommended; my claim is that it matters what overall perspective one brings to them.[26]

As for the phenomena of loving, my survey is incomplete. Not all loves are erotic or (Freud to the contrary perhaps) rooted in or tinged with the erotic. There is, of course, love of one's children and of friends, meaning in the optimal case that you identify their good with yours and care about them the way you do about yourself. Love of one's children is natural; my sense of self and its well-being extends, by an almost biological imperative, to them and theirs. Friendship is not natural in that way, though it answers to the needs of a being who is by nature social in the sense that he is unfulfilled without any close bond with another to cherish and be cherished by. Human connections of this magnitude or intensity are rare occurrences in one lifetime; you might have many warm acquaintances, but you are unlikely to have a multitude of friends. If, as Aristotle says, "One is related to [one's] friend as to himself (for his friend is another self),"[27] two consequences follow. You cannot expect to have more than a few "other selves"; friendship is, in a way, an exclusive kind of relation. And, as in the love associated with Eros, not every personality is capable of true friendship; such profound interest in another's well-being requires certain virtues. A friend is someone you can predictably rely upon, and an intemperately self-indulgent person—with little capacity to resist impulses or pleasures, and to endure the painful—is, among other things, unpredictable and undependable.

It would be foolish to extend the aforegoing case for moderation in the arena of love so far as to imply that moderation is what love is mostly about. Love is about enduring intimate attachments or devotedness; moderation, as I've contended, is a necessary precondition for that and a guide through its labyrinths. A further qualification to be noted, if not already apparent, is that the role of reasoned weighing and balancing is less prominent in the enterprise of love than in the enterprise of politics, because the former doesn't demand the exercise of power (indeed, it demands its surrender) and the latter isn't about passionate intimacies. Hence the familiar expression "moderation in all things" represents an unnuanced truth or a half-truth that points to a reality but falls short of capturing the complexities, which remain labyrinthine.

This analysis has neglected a form of love that the Christian tradition calls agape, which seems to mean love of everyone. Agape is a form of devotion transcending the one-sidedness or partisanship that infects all the others; it applies to strangers and even those who have wronged you. "You have heard that it was said, 'You shall love your neighbor [brethren, friends] and hate your enemies,' but I say to you love your enemies and pray for those who persecute you. . . . For if you love [only] those who love you, what reward have you?"[28]; anyone can do that. The injunction against hatred can be seen as a wise moderator, addressing as it does one of the greatest roots of virulent excess in human affairs. But the broader injunction to love everyone "as thyself," to do good to those who harm you, and to extend a boundless forgiveness to wrongdoers seems so sharply at variance with natural inclination as to amount to an impossibility. The demand that "you, therefore, must be perfect as your Heavenly Father is perfect" parts company with the idea of moderation, which eschews unrealistic demands for perfection. The Gospel answers such objections by pronouncing that "with God all things are possible"; as this may be read, the universality of love God requires is attainable but only with God's help bestowed upon the faithful.

In the absence of that Divine call and bestowal our lovings are always partisan, concentrated upon romantic partners, family, friends—our "loved ones" in the ordinary sense.[29] That is, they are always passions whose nurture and equilibrium are dependent upon resources merely human. With regard to those who are not our loved ones, the religion of the Bible can serve to inspire goodwill, but goodwill is something less than agape and something less than friendship. Aristotle observes that goodwill is not yet friendship, "for it does not involve intensity or desire, whereas these accompany friendly feeling [which] implies intimacy."[30]

The brief reference to goodwill invites attention to the subject of compassion, to which I cannot do full justice here but which belongs to the inquiry. Compassion is a feeling for the suffering of others which might involve intensity though, strictly speaking, is not a desire directed to the persons who are its objects and doesn't entail intimacy. Compassion, unlike love and friendship, can be widely bestowed; you can feel it for many, indeed for whole groups of people. No extended discussion is needed to show how compassion benefits our social and interpersonal relations; life would be much harsher and more painful and individuals more alien to each other without this. And, it is maintained from religious and psychiatric viewpoints, your own psychic health is improved if you can muster sympathy for those who have wronged you; anger is thereby modified before it becomes an all-consuming hatred. Stop to consider and try to empathize with what the wrongdoer has been going through and suffering; then you can forgive and be relieved of deleterious rage.

Yet the contribution of compassion to human flourishing may be exaggerated by its more enthusiastic proponents. Three points are to be made on this side of the issue, which I arrange in ascending order of importance. First, enthusiasts should be reminded that compassion has a basis in elementary self-interestedness; sometimes the individual commiserates with the suffering of another because he feels and fears that he could be subjected to the same kind of pain. "Oh, that could be me!" At the root of much commiseration expressed for putative victims of injustice is this: "I do not want to be treated that way"; I identify with whomever is a recipient of treatment from which I wish to be free. While hardly disposing of compassion as something valuable, this bit of psychological realism promotes a more sober attitude toward it.

The second point is that commiseration by itself is insufficient for the establishment of enduring bonds or deep attachments among us; it is an episodic emotion and, so to speak, a negative one. You feel it when occasions for pity come to your attention; in other words, it tends to come and go depending upon circumstances and perceptions of circumstances. An empathy for someone's suffering is not the same thing as a persistent concern for his or her well-being; I can feel bad about your pain without much positive interest in your overall flourishing. For the same reason, compassion is not a sufficient stimulus for communal bonding or public spiritedness; it cannot be relied upon to unite members of a community on a basis that is enduring.[31]

Our third point more directly confronts the relations between compassion and moderation. Note that the former is a prominent virtue in contemporary liberal thought but not in classical moral philosophy, which is one reason that classical moral philosophy sounds harsh to our ears. For example, there is no listing of compassion as such among the some thirteen moral virtues enumerated in book 2 of Aristotle's *Ethics.*[32] Why? Because it is a passion, and virtues are defined as habituated dispositions whose function it is to regulate and refine passions on behalf of reasonable outcomes. Is this emotion in need of regulation? It would not be if its outcome were always desirable and its objects always appropriate recipients of it, but one who assumes that this is the case is looking at human affairs from a rather simple and sanguinary perspective. One may have compassion for some convicted criminals, but how about serial killers or terrorists? You might suggest that all such persons are appropriate recipients of sympathy, for, after all, they are troubled human beings. But even granting that, aren't they also appropriate objects of righteous anger or indignation on account of the massive harm they have perpetrated? And if you identify sympathetically with the victims, how can you fail to share the natural anger of the victims or their survivors? Perhaps anger and compassion should be held in some kind of equilibrium, but the idea that the latter is always morally preferable to the former is an idea inconducive to moderation. To put it in terms of practical consequences: indiscriminate compassion can be harmful by weakening constraints, legal and ethical, upon wrongdoing; these salutary constraints are sustainable among many because often enough indignation outweighs sympathy for the doers of serious harm.

The broader point is that compassion, like love, is a generally benign effect in need of oversight from a reasoning element in us that exercises a discriminating judgment about what is worthy and unworthy, better and worse. As a matter of fact, most of us do choose among possible objects of commiseration (some lavishing it upon Palestinians; others upon Israelis, etc.); the trouble is that our choices are too often ill-informed, driven excessively by partisan attachments and unguided by a sober discrimination. It is a mistake then to think of compassion as the supreme virtue or as an unqualified good; it can be properly or improperly directed, and we can envision too much as well as too little of it. Finally, the underlying consideration here may be generalized: wherever there is a too much or a too little, wherever we have to face alternative pitfalls of this sort, there is a role for moderation.

My version of the case for moderation stresses the centrality of character, the essentials of which are ingrained inner discipline and outer reliability. But character is not an uncontested concept; there are differing conceptions of it and of its importance. One's view of its importance depends, to a large extent, on one's view of the human passions. My argument implies that some of our basic passions are problematic to a degree that their direction—by limitation or refinement—is a fundamental task for us all, and, as a corollary, that the desideratum of a harmonious life is no spontaneous occurrence but a project always facing difficulties. This outlook is challengeable in two opposite ways. If you think that our natural passions are wholly benign, then you might have little use for the concept of character; on the other hand, if you think that we have injurious natural impulses so powerful as to be virtually unmodifiable by any ordinary means, then character would appear as a very insufficient if not illusory answer to them. Also implicated in this divergence of outlooks is the role of reason and its prospects.

Freud's analysis of the personality takes into account the emergence of character in the psychodynamic processes by which raw impulses are restrained and redirected, but it is treated much more as a psychic reaction than a proactive ameliorative agent. The prime actors are the dangerously irrational and antisocial id, the ego (seat of our capacity to recognize reality), and the more or less oppressive superego (which has internalized harsh demands of society)—agencies in perpetual conflict. The id's primitive lusts are not only fiercely demanding, they are also intractable in the sense that you cannot do anything that would eradicate or fundamentally transform them. Insofar as amelioration is possible, it is through various psychic transactions whereby the embattled ego seeks to shift, or in the technical terminology "displace," primitive drives, diverting their energy toward objects less threatening or more in accord with society's requirements. This process is especially imperative with regard to the intense aggression that Freud (along with Nietzsche in his way) regards as a basic natural instinct; the elemental aggressive impulses cannot be eliminated, but, with luck, some of their demands can be sated by ego-inspired provisions of substitute gratification (e.g., prize fighting and football instead of mayhem and killing). Hence, and perhaps paradoxically, Freud depends significantly upon reason, of a sort, to get us through our malaise, though the project of the ego's rationality is finally to secure as much gratification of the pleasure-seeking id as is compatible with the security of the whole organism. Also paradoxical is that much of the ego's strategic maneuvering is not conducted in full consciousness (unconscious yet in the service of reasonable ends?). In this and similar outlooks our reason is portrayed as frail and forever besieged, and its work is always fragile.[33]

The Freudian ego's labyrinthine transactions with the id may be viewed as efforts to accomplish, by rather different means, the moderating function that character is thought to perform in the more traditional outlooks. Insofar as psychoanalysis seeks to bolster the ego—that part of us capable of understanding—it retains an accord with the classical teaching about the soul's well-being; also in accord with that teaching is the Freudian recognition (even at the level of ego operations) that reasoned deliberation by itself is hardly sufficient for the task of controlling impetuous passions. Neither Freud nor Aristotle would dream of entertaining the defective notion that one tempers impetuous impulses simply by remonstrating with them. Here then is the interesting psychological question: when passions are brought under control, when a degree of moderation is attained, what makes that possible? The classical view is that reason stands in need of an ally in the psyche (as it needs allies in its external or social operations). In its Aristotelian version, that ally is the ensemble of habituated dispositions regarding actions and feelings that you have acquired largely by repeatedly choosing and behaving appropriately under the guidance of socializing communal norms or educative

models. Thus, in the best cases, primal angers, fears, and lusts are tempered as they are incorporated into your character; in this way, thought
and decision may have an abiding effect upon impulses. For example,
one who has been taught that it is proper to stand up to wrongdoing
and decides to do so will feel more confident and less fearful doing so
the next time; fortitude and firmness can become part and parcel of
who you are. To anticipate an objection, the habits to which I'm refer-
ring are of course dispositions—tendencies, not automatic mechanisms.
They can be more or less reasonable as the norms superintending their
development are more or less reasonable, and they can promote practical wisdom in that the next time one is in a better position to make an
insightful choice.

Is this a superficial view of the matter? It would be chargeable as such
if the irrational forces were as powerful and, at bottom, intransigent as
Freud thought them to be; then choices and habits would appear as phenomena on the surface of life without any profound effect on the depths.
The orientation one can call Aristotelian or classical allows that we are
indeed creatures with irrational passions that cause persistent problems,
because they are resistant to deliberate alteration. But they are not wholly
intransigent; in varying degrees, and sometimes to a large degree, they
can be shaped by efforts collective and individual.[34]

What the two versions of human nature just noted have in common
can be highlighted by their contrast with a third. In some post-Freudian
psychologies, our natural inclinations are perceived as relatively unprob-
lematic, with the consequence that self-restraint as a requisite of well-
being is downgraded. Indeed, restraint is held to be a part of the problem,
and often a large part of it; we impose certain artificial constraints, social
and psychological, upon ourselves by which spontaneity is suppressed
and the natural healthy growth of personality is inhibited. From such
a perspective "character" may be seen as a peripheral phenomenon and
even as an undesirable one. In their book *Gestalt Therapy: Excitement
and Growth in the Human Personality*, psychologists Perls, Hefferline, and
Goodman offer this observation:

> Self-conquest is normally esteemed as "character." A man of character
> does not succumb to "weakness" (this weakness actually is the sponta-

neous *Eros* that accomplishes all creation). He can marshall his aggression to put over his "ideals" (ideals are the norms one is resigned to). . . . But grace, warmth, strength, good sense, gaiety, tragedy: these are impossible to the man of character.[35]

In fairness we should note that what is meant by self-conquest here is a rigidly authoritarian self which, with the aid of internal aggressiveness, seeks to ride roughshod over everything else in the psyche, because it is unwilling and afraid to recognize its human vulnerabilities. But of considerable interest is the fact that these authors choose to name this condition, which they regard as a virulent pathology, "character."

Though retaining aspects of the Freudian model, Perls and his associates present a picture of the human condition in some respects at the opposite end of the modern psychiatric spectrum. That this picture has a kind of liberal and democratic appeal is a further reason for exploring it. At its core is the idea of "growth." The organism exists in an environment of ever-changing possibilities; the healthy condition is one of awareness and openness to them, and hence continuing inclination to venture into new "contacts," which will result in reconfiguration of the self.[36] Growth's opposite, neurosis, is such a fixation on an unchangeable past condition as to preclude the awareness of possibility. The neurotic is fixated because he or she is afraid of reconfiguration and of reopening old and unresolved conflicts. This idea that obsessive fixation upon past events is at the root of pathology might be considered Freudian, but the following elaboration much less so.

> We are saying, then, that neurosis does not consist in any active conflict, inner or outer, of one desire against another, or of social standards against animal needs, or of personal needs (e.g., ambition) against both social standards or animal needs. All such conflicts are compatible with the integration of the self, and indeed are means of integrating the self.[37]

The clear implication is that these conflicts are not all that troublesome; they do not permanently divide the personality, and they are alleviated, if not left behind, as one resolves to "grow" by moving on to new contacts in one's social environment. Underlying this relative optimism is the idea that the personality, or the self, is basically creative; the external entities one "contacts" are not simply objective realities but are to a large degree realities whose meanings one creates. At this point the concept of contacting gets rather complicated, perhaps a bit murky.

Gestalt psychology should be accorded its due. It gives rise to valuable therapeutic insights that are also consistent with common sense—for example, inner malaise is often subject to amelioration by outward actions that maintain and increase one's social involvements. Philosophically, in its recognition that we are social beings and its claim that a person ordinarily retains some capacity to make effectual choices if he or she can muster the courage to do so, this psychology reminds us of aspects of the Aristotelian tradition. And our contemporaries may find attractive the importance accorded to inherent personal creativity and the liberation from Freudian emphasis upon the determination of past events.

But can the outlook under consideration dispense with the concept of moderation? Occasionally our Gestalt authors acknowledge a "conservative" need of the organism to preserve aspects of its present identity as it progressively ventures into ever new territories, but the progressive desideratum is what really counts. (On the analogy of a sporting event, I would have to say that the progressives defeat the conservatives by a score of 3 to 1.) This is an emphatically forward-looking account of how the psyche functions and prospers.[38] It is also, at base, a rather sanguine account, supposing that the great human contradictions, "inner or outer," with which thinkers from Platonists to Freudians have wrestled, are resolvable with little need for an enduring authoritative agency, inner or outer, whose function is to direct the resolution. In other words, its tendency is to be sanguine about the emotions—the beneficence of our "spontaneous *Eros*"—and therefore suspicious of restraints, including restraints imposed habitually and by moral character.

The idea that personality develops through the experience and incorporation of connections with others is a sensible one as far as it goes, but the other side of wisdom is full recognition of the fact that not all contacts are good ones; some could be quite bad for you. (The hapless protagonist in *Of Human Bondage* has made quite a bad one.) How is a personality constituted so that the better is regularly preferred and chosen over the worse? Unless one has nearly boundless confidence in the beneficence of our natural Eros, it's hard to see how the consistent (as distinguished from the unreliably episodic) rejection of the unworthy in favor of the worthy is to be expected without some stable, authoritative inner regulation conducive thereto. And the existence of such consistent self-regulation is difficult to envision without the aid of habits sufficiently ingrained as to be usually resistant to change.

In theories as well as in ordinary living, tensions can easily arise between the desiderata of a tempering habituation and of openness to change. No doubt the former can be carried to such extremes as to preclude grace, warmth, and gaiety; focusing upon this undesirable outcome, progressivist or liberationist psychologies tend to place heavy emphasis upon openness at the expense of character development. But, even apart from the moral question of worthy and unworthy choices, who would really want to be so wide open and hence changeable as to lack stability, continuity, or firmness in one's experience of life and dealings with others? The idea of moderation suggests that, with regard to both of these ingredients of personality, you can have too much or too little. In the development of a healthy equilibrium between them, it seems evident that the grounds of stability and continuity have to be established first.[39]

Character, I've asserted, is a necessary condition for both the practical purposes of well-being and the theoretical purposes of understanding human nature and conduct. But that it is a necessary condition doesn't mean that it is a sufficient condition for either of these purposes. As to practical flourishing, and insofar as this includes a coherent life, what resources do you have to ensure that your various habits will cohere in a tolerable harmony (integration or unity of some sort being implied in the very notion of having a character)? As to the theoretical concern, character, while critical, hardly suffices as a total definition of the person. Of course, there is also your "personality," in the narrower sense of the term; for example, are you pleasingly outgoing, optimistic, and interesting? Personality is perhaps a greater contributor to worldly success than moralists might think it ought to be, but let us leave it aside in favor of a factor more philosophically pertinent.

Being a person includes the potentiality for reflection upon one's character, judging it, wishing for an improvement, or simply observing that it is "mine"—that this is "how I am." Our capacity for introspection, if meaningful, points to some aspect of the soul, which, being in a position to observe one's characteristic attributes, somehow transcends them; what is this transcendent element, and how, if at all, are we to explain it?

One kind of answer is that there exists a real or authentic "self," which, while often obscured by the persona I've sent out into the world or by accommodations made to social forms, somehow underlies all the habits I've acquired. But questions abound on this subject of what constitutes a person's identity. Isn't it a simplicity, and a rather romantic one, to suppose that a real me, so to speak, exists in there awaiting discovery? Perls and his associates reject any such notion and offer this alternative: "The advice 'be yourself' that is often given by therapists is somewhat absurd; what is meant is 'contact the actuality,' for the self is only that contact."[40] Your self at any moment is the aggregate of your contacts; therefore, it is always fluid and unfinished, emerging or receding as contacts are made, changed, or refused. It would follow that the task is less a matter of "finding yourself" than a matter of assertive creating—that is, ever-changeable exercises of volition. This way of looking at it, while interesting, is not without its own difficulties. In view of all this fluidity, the question of "who am I?" becomes a perplexity indeed, even more so than in most other theories. Usually when we think of personal identity, we are thinking of something enduring.

If the self is not adequately definable either as a real me or as an ever-changing process or as an assertion of will, then how are we to define it? The answer would seem to be that it is not fully definable. I have no wish to denigrate psychological inquiries concerned with this concept; they can be more or less illuminating. The conclusion is hard to avoid that there is something inhabiting a psyche that is the locus of a person's distinctive individuality, or the sense one has of distinct individuality. This phenomenon seems insufficiently accounted for by one's character; we might as well call it the self. (When lovers unite psychologically we do not envision that it is the union only of two moral characters; Donne called it "two soules.") My main point here is that the self is more easily felt than analyzed; there is and will always be elusiveness about it. We might as well say, with Jewish theologian Abraham Heschel: "As a person [man] is both a mystery and a surprise."[41]

One rather mysterious phenomenon is that you can have dialogue with yourself, yet this is an undoubtable fact—you do that often enough. The inner discourse may consist of questions and answers, arguments and counterarguments, even self-condemnation and self-justification. Now what is talking to what or who to whom? This essential reality, both familiar and strange, resists clear conceptualization. It is susceptible of various depictions, yet regarding its basis or precondition—what makes it possible—some accounts of the human condition may be preferred to others. Dialogue in the soul is apparently better accounted for by reference to rationality than by reference to creative volition. The idea that we are rational beings entails something more than that we are simply calculating beings who can deliberate about the means to our ends; also entailed is that our thinking is inherently self-conscious. Whatever else might be said about human reason, the capacity for subjective reflexivity has to be considered a defining feature. (Arguably my cat and my computer engage in some cognitive activities, but they are not self-conscious about that.) Also arguable is that this cognitive capacity of ours, when it affects conduct, does so with a bias in favor of consistency or coherence, which is the bias of the intellect. Perhaps it would be too much to say that the reflexive component of reason fully explains the sense you have of an "I," somehow distanced from the ensemble of your characteristic inclinations, which can observe them and, under favorable conditions, facilitate a coherent volition with regard to them. But if our pervasive experience of reflexivity is to be credited as evidential, that goes some way toward an explanation.

Self-consciousness, with its potentiality for inner dialogue, is no guarantee of moderation; after all, the dialogue might be inconclusive or even infected by the very irrational elements in need of regulation. Self-consciousness is not necessarily a successful moderator, but it is a critical contributor insofar as it allows for a psychological distancing and relatively dispassionate awareness of one's proclivities and problems.

The distancing capacity, as I would call it, is the object of considerable interest in contemporary psychology, especially among those concerned with the subject of emotional intelligence. Psychologist Daniel Goleman writes: "Psychologists use the rather ponderous term *metacognition* to refer to an awareness of [one's] thought processes, and *metamood* to mean awareness of one's own emotion. I prefer the term *self-awareness* in the sense of an ongoing attention to one's internal states."[42] This attention can take the form of an impartial observation conducted with equanimity. Goldman continues:

> At its best, self-observation allows . . . an equanimous awareness of passionate or turbulent feelings. At a minimum, it manifests itself simply as a slight stepping-back from experience, a parallel stream of consciousness that is "meta": hovering above or beside the main flow, aware of what is happening rather than being immersed and lost in it. It is the difference between, for example, being murderously enraged at someone and having the self-reflexive thought "this is anger I'm feeling" even as you are enraged . . . This awareness of emotions is the fundamental emotional competence on which others, such as emotional self-control, build.[43]

Most relevant to the theoretical point I've just been making is that researchers like Goleman find evidence for the existence of the "meta" phenomenon—an aspect of the mind's functioning which allows it, sometimes, to reflect, in a manner approaching objectivity, upon its own functioning and affects. Goleman is less interested in this phenomenon's implications for a philosophy of human nature than he is in its practical uses, its efficacy in the management of an array of problematic emotive conditions: anger, anxiety, melancholy, or depression. In all such cases awareness is the indispensable first step and basis for interventions that forestall the escalation of these conditions to their pathological extremities. For example, the mind can preclude the escalation of an "anger cycle" by recognizing its early stages and intervening early on before it becomes a crescendo of uncontrollable rage. If you catch it soon enough you can reappraise the perceptions or misperceptions that triggered the anger, and you can arrange distractions from it.

This practical insight brings us welcome news from the world of psychological research about the potentialities of thought. But it might be a bit too sanguine regarding our ability to regulate passions by thinking about them. As Goleman is inclined to acknowledge, the strategies he recommends are most effective when dealing with the ordinary, garden-variety emotional difficulties; for the severe cases, medication or psychotherapy might be needed. Largely missing from this analysis is the importance of character as mediator between cognition and passion. Our habitual dispositions—with regard to anger, fear, and desires of all sorts—significantly affect our perceptions; while "awareness" is an essential aspect of our human equipment, the degree of its availability to someone depends on his or her characteristic inclinations in the face of threats, temptations, and the like. In other words, whether and how much you can distance yourself from upsurges of anger or fear is contingent upon whether or how much you have acquired a character through which these passions have been tempered. Where there is defective character development, small frustrations can appear to be huge ones because you are not prepared to tolerate them, and rage can foreclose the chance of detached reflection. Perhaps an adequate degree of character development is presupposed when Goleman relies upon "equanimous awareness"; at any rate, what he regards as "the fundamental emotional competence" is in need of some help.[44]

Regarding the concept of emotional intelligence (E.I.), what I find most intriguing is that it is an effort to identify and explore a certain kind of wisdom about successful living. In some respects, as I've briefly suggested, the intelligence explored might be viewed as akin to that practical wisdom which Aristotle famously linked to experience, as distinguished from theoretical knowledge or abstract cognition. E.I. is represented as a mode of thinking that is closely connected to feelings and which draws upon them; Goleman speaks of "the emotional wisdom garnered through past experiences." Maybe that is why its discussants and proponents prefer to identify it as an "awareness" more often than they identify it as reasoning or rationality. Yet as intelligence it has to be considered an exercise of the rational faculties—a way of understanding and knowing. What Aristotle and E.I. proponents are talking about is often observable in ordinary affairs: you are acquainted with persons who, while not highly educated or learned, have insight—concerning emotions, and more broadly, concerning vicissitudes of life—and whom you would consult about your well-being more readily than you would consult some others with advanced academic degrees. These practically insightful psychologists and moralists may stand as testimony for the claim that there is such a thing as wisdom about human affairs, nonscientific though it may be.[45]

We find emotional intelligence linked often enough to moderation. Goleman writes: "The goal is balance, not emotional suppression. . . . As Aristotle observed, what is wanted is *appropriate* emotion, feeling proportionate to circumstances."[46] Feelings belong to our natural equipment for living; their suppression is pathological, but so too are their excesses. Anger and even anxiety have their uses, while too much debilitates and immobilizes.

Are these propositions, and their likes, practical truths about human flourishing as such, or are they, as a thoroughgoing ethical relativism might insist, only opinions no better than the alternative opinions about what is good and bad for us? Of course they can be challenged; Nietzsche would think little of them, and they are not Romantic. Yet they have held up rather well over time despite differences in cultures. A personality driven by uncontrollable rages or helpless because of uncontrollable fear is in a recognizably pathological condition; to deny that this judgment has any universal validity is in effect to doubt that there is any psychopathology anywhere. And to affirm this judgment is to acknowledge, at least, that balance is a desideratum of import.

No doubt an element of relativity is introduced insofar as "feeling proportionate to circumstances" is what we mean by balance. In the previous chapter I discussed prudential insight as an ingredient of political moderation, and so it is with regard to personal moderation. At whom shall I be angry, or of whom afraid, and under what provocations and how much? Obviously this question is answerable only with a view to particular circumstances or situations, therefore leaving latitude for differing judgment calls about what is proportional and what is excessive here and now. In the most exigent cases (terrorism, for example), the answer might be clear-cut, but in more ordinary affairs (who is largely to blame in the marital breakup; how serious really was the provocation that led to an altercation, etc.) there is often room for disagreement, even among practically wise observers. Yet there is less room for disagreement about what kind of character is needed—what kind of person you need to become—in order to be able to make such judgment calls reflectively. Uncertainties accompany one's situational assessment of appropriateness in response to a specific provocation or temptation, but who does not see that impulse control is a desideratum much affecting the possibility of any thoughtful assessment?

The potentiality we have for dialogue in the soul is no guarantee that the soul will be temperate, because reasoning and moderation of character are not the same thing, as a thought and a habit are not the same thing. But the different capacities are related in two ways. Our habituations may reflect judicious social norms that were influential in their formation, and an inner discipline of impetuous passions, or a cultivated balance among the psyche's affective demands, allows for the exercise of balanced thinking. On these grounds, common sense envisions the existence of more or less reasonable habits. (For example, a drug habit is neither informed by nor hospitable to thoughtfulness, but a cultivated disposition to fortitude in the face of pain or danger can be thus informed and hospitable.) To put it differently, and in the language of an ancient philosophic controversy, wisdom and virtue do not amount to the same thing, but they need and support each other.

As for the question about one's personal "identity," I have raised it because psychological exploration of our subject matter eventually gives rise to it. This is not a particularly Aristotelian question, as the self is not a focus of Aristotelian inquiry.[47] Yet, while lacking the temerity to attempt a systematic definition of all that constitutes your identity, I am arguing, as the Aristotelian tradition suggests, that your character constitutes the most substantial element of who you are.

As for harmony and disharmony, we have noted a Nietzschean case for disorder in the psyche: inner tension is the condition and the incentive for vital striving and creativity; lack of inner tension or refusal to experience it means complacency and stolid mediocrity. Let us accept what there is of truth in this claim; after all, there is diversity and distance in the soul by nature, and at critical junctures in a lifetime one is much better off experiencing and coming to grips with self-contradictions. Hence there is such a thing as being too comfortable with oneself, as is "the last man" and as is his cousin, the easygoing nonjudgmentalist. But who wants chaos inside; who wants a psyche whose incessant divergences make it a perpetual battleground?

Finally, if you want to be basically one person (an identity) and not several, ever in contradiction and vacillation, then value the contribution that moderation makes to wholeness. And if friendship and love are human goods, then appreciate the trustworthiness that depends upon moderation.

Chapter 3

Philosophical Moderation
Tempering the Mind

I have sought to test and justify the idea of moderation through confrontation and dialogue with several modern (and psychologically oriented) outlooks on the human condition—Nietzschean, Romantic, Freudian, progressive post-Freudian—which are remote from the philosophic origins of the idea and would seem to pose sizeable challenges to it. Though in substance these perspectives are diverse, they have one element in common and which they share with the viewpoint I am maintaining: each one, in its own way, yields judgments about better and worse, healthy and unhealthy, states of personality. That is, each one entails some conception or other of what constitutes human flourishing, and so we can envision a dialogue with and among them.

We can also envision something like the following response from a modernistic or postmodern point of view, radically skeptical and relativistic: "This project is a misguided one; you are wrong in supposing that there is such a thing as *human flourishing* to have a dialogue about. In fact no defensible foundation exists for any judgments about what is better and worse, even healthy and unhealthy, for mankind as such. Reasoning cannot supply any foundation because, in the final analysis, all evaluations about what is good for us are products of subjective opinions dictated by one's personality, one's culture, or both. Your conclusions can seem plausible only if your underlying assumptions about our humanity are accepted as true, but these are truths not discovered but constructed, ultimately invented, and they do not acquire validity simply because, as many have been induced to believe them, they pass as common sense. This has to be the case because an objective understanding of reality is unavailable. You might as well have recourse to religious visions and biblical stories."

I have responded to aspects of this critique from time to time, but without a sufficiently systematic focus on its basic claims and its own assumptions. Let us note at the outset that what follows from it is that a case for moderation can have no more general validity than a case for vitalistic immoderation, and a harmonious balance in the psyche is in reality no more of a good thing than chaos in the psyche. Let us come to grips with the central concepts and attitudes that entail such conclusions. This inquiry will lead us further on to exploration of what several of the most interestingly pertinent moral philosophers have had to say on our topic.

Every vision of our fulfillment can be traced finally to some conception of what we are; call it human nature or the kind of being that is human. Cultural relativists are bent upon showing and emphasizing the great variety of ways of being human, while denigrating ideas of uniformity or normality for our species as a whole. The current mantra is that all such ideas, including those purporting to be analytic or contemplative, are necessarily "social constructs"—reflections of the way people happen to live in one or another of the diverse (parochial) cultures. For example, in the West we practice and therefore extol monogamy, with the values it entails, whereas in other places they practice and extol polygamy, and a moral philosophy arguing the worthiness of the former would be dismissible as rationalization of ethnocentric preference. Postmodern doctrines incorporate cultural relativism while adding to it relentless attacks upon rationality and the prospects for genuine knowledge about trans-subjective realities. This critique prominently claims that thought, however abstract, is determined by social and political interests, especially by the location of one's group in a social hierarchy (class, race, and gender are the current determinants in vogue). More pointedly, theories and speculations about life and its problems are said to be constructed in the service of power; the thing to do with them is "deconstruction," that is, disclosing their implicit justifications for the exercise of power by those who have it or its acquisition by those who don't. The autonomy of the mind—its capacity for nonpartisan inquiries and conclusions—is emphatically debunked.[1] Indeed, none of the substantive perspectives I've discussed in these essays would survive the acids of this reductionism (not even those affirming the preeminent value of the irrational), because they all claim to have some hold on the truth. But perhaps moderation is the greatest casualty, insofar as its practice requires a reliance on cognitive wisdom and its justification requires systematic argument.

As to cultural relativism, anthropologists who stress the variety of ways of life do have a point, but the point can be exaggerated; pushed to its utmost conclusion it amounts to a claim that everything important about us is attributable to (diverse) cultural conditionings and nothing of importance is attributable to our (common) nature. Though cultural relativists often sound as if they think this way, we rarely hear from them an explicit argument going so far as this. Precisely speaking, to deny the existence of a common humanity is to assert that there is literally nothing good or desirable for human beings per se. Such a position cannot be maintained with thoroughgoing consistency.

Ordinary relativists seldom deny that preservation of one's life and the experience of more pleasure than suffering are natural wants. And, although culture certainly conditions the form of the family, it is acknowledged that virtually everywhere in the world there exists a family or kinship structure that is cherished. More extensive communal bonds are discoverable almost everywhere; furthermore friendship and love exist as desiderata in diverse cultures. If these are commonplaces, they are commonplaces with implications. All of these desiderata and commitments—family, community, friendship, love—depend upon the exercise of some constraints upon elementary self-centered passions; they are incompatible with unlimited self-assertion or indulgence. To be sure, these factors are shaped in different ways among different peoples, but what society and what "culture" regularly admire the perpetual drunk or a person unable to commit energetically to any serious purpose, cooperate in a communal project, or care about anyone or anything beyond personal gratification?

Cultural relativists themselves are not entirely relativistic; underlying their efforts to rebut claims about things normative or generally valid for mankind, one can discern a value judgment—a judgment against ethnocentric thinking, that is, in favor of open-mindedness and tolerance of difference. Anthropologist Clifford Geertz, a leading proponent of that position, puts it this way: "What relativists, so called, want us to worry about is provincialism—the danger that our perceptions will be dulled, our intellects constricted and our sympathies narrowed by the overlearned and overvalued acceptances of our own society."[2] Geertz does not explore why intellectual constriction and narrow sympathies are bad things; is it simply because they are so regarded by the provincial norms of the culture that has nurtured modern Western anthropologists? That would not be much of a basis for their indictment. Perhaps constricted minds and sympathies are to be considered as disabilities undesirable per se; if so, are these the only disabilities subject to that kind of evaluation? What about lack of self-control and consequent unreliability and a psyche driven by chaotic divisions? To put it in positive terms, once you have deemed that open-mindedness and toleration are valid norms transculturally, you are hard put to exclude from consideration other claims to that status, including claims on behalf of moderation.

It seems to me that, doctrinally, the greater threat to the idea of moderation arises from the postmodernist attack upon reason and knowledge. To state the point most simply, one who has no respect for reason is ill-disposed to listen to argument, entertain viewpoints differing from those one currently holds, and cultivate that capacity for deliberation that is part and parcel of a self-controlling character. Less simply put, an ethic of restraint and balance is particularly in need of an ideational climate favorable to it, because that ethic makes demands upon us that are resisted by primal urges and desires. While the qualities of moderation may be indispensable to our well-being in the long run, we are not spontaneously attracted to them; real appreciation for them comes after a more or less demanding habituation and education. Hence moderation stands in need of a persuasive, systematic rationale that can indicate why self-discipline and balance are both salutary and possible. That enterprise cannot be taken seriously where reason is disrespected.

Under the postmodernist impulse, one is inclined to denigrate any such enterprise as covertly partisan, rooted in special interests. For example, a rationale for an ethic of self-restraint could be deconstructed as an ideology arising from and supporting bourgeois class interests, its real object being the promotion of attitudes or personalities conducive to capitalist productivity, bourgeois law and order, and the power of property owners. (This notion could have some merit if it were not the case that the idea of moderation is at least as old as Socratic philosophy, which also took a critical view of wealth-seeking and the rich.[3]) Insofar as the case for moderation makes an argument on behalf of disinterested reflection, it is beset with assertions that no one can authentically do that, and the belief in it is at best an illusion. As the expression goes, "Everyone is coming from somewhere," which seems to mean that where you come from inexorably dictates what you must be and think, and no one, even the "truth-seeking" scientist or philosopher, can rise above that.

The concept that thinking is biased by the thinker's personality and background is not a recent discovery. The persons Socrates encounters in Platonic dialogues assert opinions that reflect their (diverse) personalities, backgrounds, or aspirations, and the encounters are designed to show the attentive reader both how difficult it is to make them entertain challenges to their received opinions *and* that it is sometimes possible to do so. Platonic dialogues recognize that everyone *is* coming from somewhere, but that where you are going is, at least on occasion and with the right person, open to effectual discussion.

If Plato is wrong and radical postmodernists are right, that is bad news for liberal education, which seeks, among other things, to get received opinions challenged from perspectives broader or deeper than those with which the student arrived. Why bother to do that if you already know that ideas and arguments are always products of the social class, race, or gender of those who maintain them, and that the most important thing to know about a philosophy is whose power it rationalizes and serves. Postmodern deconstructionists might believe that they are promoting a spirit of questioning by unmasking and debunking traditional thought, but their doctrines have the effect of discouraging genuine inquiry and rendering the injunction "know thyself" virtually meaningless. Indeed if you were persuaded of the validity of their doctrines (despite your middle-class upbringing), why wouldn't you reject the enterprise of thoughtful dialogue in favor of the enthusiastic reaffirmation of whatever you already feel and believe? This outcome, interestingly, is at a variance with the open-mindedness that some cultural relativists wish to promote.[4]

But why accept the view that the mind is without autonomy because its operations are always in the grip of partisan interests, especially power-seeking interests? One can easily acknowledge that this is often the case, but that it is inevitably the case is a proposition undemonstrated by postmodernists, who, to demonstrate it, would have to show us that they have engaged in at least one reasonably impartial analysis—an inquiry and argument not wholly biased by their own group orientation or power-seeking aspirations. Put differently, if the basic thesis is that all thought about the human condition is necessarily dictated by ideological preferences and partiality, how do you confidently arrive at this conclusion, and convince others to take it seriously, without having pursued the kind of objective inquiry that you say is impossible? If you can't, if your postmodern outlook is as much ideology as all the rest, then it would seem that the game is up.

A postmodernist might respond as follows: "This is a trick of the sort conservative rationalists are ever ready to spring. Of course my skeptical orientation is in the service of my preferences and values; what makes it better than the other ideologies is that I'm aware of this fact and do not hide it." I don't see how this helps much; the crucial question is not the postmodernist's subjective honesty but whether and how he or she can claim to have discovered a truth about our inevitable situation after doing so much to show there isn't any. As far as I can tell, that epistemological question is not adequately addressed. At this point, however, the epistemological consideration can usefully give way to a moral one about the value preferences underlying and activating this outlook.

The postmodernist depreciation of rationality is also an assault upon norms or standards—social, political, ethical, as well as those affirmed by moral philosophy, which are dissolved under the acids of a critique that pronounces them to be groundless if not fraudulent. The reality putatively disclosed, and indeed embraced, by this undertaking is that of a normless world. What interests could be served or what vision of the desirable is supported by this view of the world? The vision suggesting itself, discernible at the base of it all, is of a limitless freedom—no normative limits or constraints whatever upon any personal inclinations. The interest served by the enthusiastic demolition of every conceivable basis for normativity is that of a boundless autonomy, and the moral ideology supported is an ultra-libertarianism; as Dostoevsky put it (disapprovingly), "Everything is permitted." You are free to do and enjoy and be anything you like, for there is no foundation in human nature or anywhere else for respectable standards of the good, the worthy, the decent, the desirable that could provide direction and set boundaries.

Another ideological interest served by this nihilism is that of a boundless equality. The demolition of all norms serves to delegitimate any preferences for some lifestyles as against others. You couldn't make a case for privileging monogamy over polygamy, or a loving commitment over promiscuous sexuality, or a self-disciplined personality over a self-indulgent one; all are equal, that is, equally unsusceptible of rational preference. So it makes sense to say that the postmodernists' underlying vision of limitless freedom is also a vision of limitless equality. Yet this outlook does not entail any affirmation, let alone defense, of equality as a mandatory ethical principle. Some contemporary liberals maintain that equal respect is a categorical imperative;[5] it should be evident why postmodernist theorizing doesn't and can't take that route. In a milieu literally devoid of normativity, there are of course no imperatives; anything goes.

Infidelities and disloyalties—why not? Pedophilia—why not? Sadism of various sorts—why not? You could say that these are extreme examples chosen to cast the postmodern project in an unattractive light, but you can speak meaningfully of extremity only if you can have recourse to a defensible idea of what is not extreme. For judgments of that kind we need signposts, and all the signposts have been removed; in a normless world it is prejudice alone that could lead to the labeling of something—a mode of conduct or of thinking—as "excessive" or "too much." (So—why not be full of prejudice? That is another question.)

Insofar as utmost personal autonomy is the desideratum envisioned by postmodern theorizing, that theorizing has another problem. Postmodernists can hardly speak of the autonomy of the mind and its liberty of thought, since they do what they can to portray thinking as subservient to nonrational forces. The alternative is a liberation of the feelings and passions; everything to which these might incline and thus every preference is permissible, in a kind of equal-opportunity hedonism. Whether this may be considered as a real autonomy is an issue for moral philosophy and psychology.

Clearly the aspiration to a boundless freedom of the latter sort is at sharp variance with the idea of moderation. Even prior to any of my arguments, it is evident that moderation is a norm, dependent upon norms and constraints external and internal to the self, and this normativity stands, one may plausibly suspect, as the special target of deconstructive endeavors.

You may reply that the issues cannot be disposed of so easily. One way to get more deeply into them is to revisit Nietzsche; that is an inquiry invited, if not mandated, by our encounters with contemporary cultural relativism and the current academic notion that reason is subservient to power.

The relevant Nietzschean proposition is that "truths" are products of our own creation; the proposition encompasses all ideas, not only about what is worthy or valuable but also about what is actual or real in this world. Concepts of nature and humanity can only be interpretations, and interpretations are "perspectives," and perspectives are activated by passions ultimately organized (when they are organized) by that volitional assertion he called "will to power." If an idea is accepted as commonsensically valid, that is because its origins have been forgotten. But whatever the origins might be, can't one try (as my second chapter does) to weigh diverse interpretations of life so as to arrive at a reasonably impartial view of their relative validity? No, because all weighing would have to be perspectival, and if you think that you have risen above partiality, you are enveloped in a fiction.

Nietzsche proclaims that "perspective" is "the basic condition of all life";[6] it is an inescapable fact, and it is more than that. "[E]very living thing can become healthy, strong and fruitful only within a horizon; if it is incapable of drawing a horizon around itself [or unable] to restrict its vision to the limits of a horizon drawn by another, it will wither away feebly or over hastily to its early demise";[7] that is, it will be devitalized. Literally, a horizon is the boundary or limit of one's vision; our intellectual and moral horizons are viewpoints from which much of reality has been excluded, and within which, therefore, some things are highlighted and brought into sharp focus. In this condition you can commit yourself wholly to a goal, a value, or a love because multifarious competing goals, values, or loves have been screened out. "No painter will paint his picture, no general achieve his victory, no people will attain its freedom without having first desired and striven for it" under inspiration provided by some limited and limiting orientation that allows for this enterprise to seem all-important.[8] Too much knowledge is a dangerous thing; a thoroughly sober and balanced picture of reality (if one could be had) would serve to show the devoted person that what he is devoted to is but one value among many in a world of ever-changing, ephemeral valuations. The conclusion that would have to be drawn from comprehensive and disinterested understanding is this: nothing is all-important, and there is no basis for a full commitment to anything. For Nietzsche, the result of horizonless or perspectiveless life would be nihilism and its personification, the apathetic "last man."

In Nietzsche's insistence on the primacy and inescapability of what he calls perspective, two claims are embodied. One bears upon the character of thought or knowledge, exposing its roots and its limitations; the other bears upon action and achievement, asserting a necessary precondition for wholehearted endeavors. These two claims are intertwined. Our knowledge is necessarily biased, one-sided; so also is the impetus of any thriving active project. Yet their implications are such as to render them susceptible to somewhat distinct inquiries.

Horizons are all man-made, some are provided for us by cultures, some by nations and empires, some by religious or other mythologies, and some are the inventions of powerfully imaginative individuals. In other words, interpretations of reality that purport to be true but aren't constitute the premises not only for our own beliefs and conduct but also for our reflections, including reflections about "human nature." The situation Nietzsche portrays resembles Plato's famous Allegory of the Cave, with this difference: the allegory supposes that beyond the cave of mere opinion there are truths of universal validity, including an idea of the good, which in some degree are available to those contemplative minds deserving to be called philosophic. The allegory, like Nietzsche, teaches skepticism about a great deal of what passes for truth, but Nietzsche seems yet more skeptical; from him we are impelled to conclude that there is nothing outside of the cave, and no one can emerge from it, insofar as that would mean a clear understanding of fundamental things as they really are. Moreover, for Nietzsche, philosophy is not essentially a contemplative enterprise but a self-assertive one; what the philosopher puts forth as discovery about reality is actually a formulation of his perspective that he desires to impose on reality. Every important philosopher has been a profoundly inventive artist who has produced a comprehensive vision of what he wants the world to be, especially what he wants, or wills, "the Good" to mean, thereby projecting a form upon formless "nature." Thus are Plato and other great artist-thinkers located among the creators of grand horizons: "Philosophy always creates the world in its own image; it cannot do otherwise. Philosophy is this tyrannical drive itself, the most spiritual will to power, to 'the creation of the world.'"[9]

Nietzsche can be said to debunk philosophic inquiry insofar as it purports to be reasoned inquiry, while admiring it insofar as it is inventive. The critique would seem to depend, at least, upon one ontological insight—that the world or "being" is without order, that it is chaotic— and upon one psychological insight—that the mind (or more exactly, the will) is, or can be, powerfully creative. The ontological reality, if fully recognized, bodes ill for human aspiration and achievement, but the creative capability may come, at times with inspiration, to our rescue. Nietzsche must purport to know somehow that these are the primary actualities and that therefore reason cannot be the agency coming to our rescue.

If philosophy is never an authentic search for understanding but must be an exercise of perspectival will, what of Nietzsche's philosophy? Does the "will to power" only represent Nietzsche's effort to create the world in his own image, or is it offered as a basic truth about natural impulse that somehow escapes the limitations he attributes to all theories (even scientific ones)?[10] Nietzsche himself raises this question: "Supposing that this also is only interpretation—and you will be eager enough to make this objection—well, so much the better."[11] So much the better? This is deliberate paradox; paradoxes can be provocatively instructive, but what are we to make of this one? Perhaps Nietzsche wants us to struggle with it; my struggle proceeds as follows. If in this passage Nietzsche means by "interpretation" what he usually means by it, why should we be impressed with his inventive self-assertion any more than Plato's inventive self-assertion? (Could Nietzsche be claiming superiority because his will is stronger?) Alternatively, suppose that Nietzsche means something closer to what is often signified by the term "perspective": an outlook which is partial in the sense that it could illuminate no more than part of the truth. But if the point is that Nietzsche's perspective has some access to the realities, that claim can be made for others; then the enterprise of truth-seeking is not precluded, though it might be rendered more modest or more dialectical by the awareness that no one can presume to have grasped the whole of it.[12]

Furthermore, despite his profound contributions to moral relativism, Nietzsche is hardly a thoroughgoing nonjudgmentalist. His works exhibit at least this pervasive affirmation about better and worse human conditions: it is worthy or healthy to have strong, spirited aspirations and devotions, and to be without aspirations or devotions beyond the immediately comfortable is unworthy complacency and enervation. This is not exactly the same vision as that boundless liberation of personal impulses and affects to which I have referred; it involves submission to a discipline that constrains some inclinations in order that others may be elevated to the station of all-important values. In the case of those Nietzsche regards as outstanding individuals, the discipline and the values are self-imposed, but one is mistaken to locate him, on this account, squarely and unqualifiedly in the camp of his most radical postmodern descendants. Differently put, Nietzsche is not the philosopher of "anything goes" that you or your culture might happen to like. He is the philosopher of a demanding spiritedness; what is to be admired is energetic commitment, which is, at its pinnacle, self-creative. If this is Nietzsche's morality (or "morality"), the philosophic question returns: how does he know this, or how does he come by it, and upon what basis are we to recognize its validity?[13]

Strangely perhaps, Nietzsche does help us to see certain psychological realities of ordinary life more sharply—especially as to preconditions for purposeful and dedicated action. His idea of horizons presents in an illuminating way this reality: vigorous practical devotion to a "cause" seems necessarily to involve a concentration of the mind upon your cause at the expense of many considerations alternative or challenging to it; you are, as Nietzsche asserts, in the grip of an orientation, a world interpretation, that renders the challenges invisible or insignificant. The point is applicable to major political and social movements, whether conservative, liberal, or radical. People ardently engaged in a campaign for civil rights are not of a mind to entertain ideas contrary to their underlying premise that "all men are created equal" and endowed with inalienable rights; for successful action these premises must be taken for granted, notwithstanding that alternative views of the subject are intellectually arguable. In any wholehearted endeavor, one takes for granted that something—a goal, an ideal, a principle—is of compelling importance; one is not open-minded about competing goals, ideals, or principles. The insight to which Nietzsche leads us is that wherever you have wholehearted commitments and strivings you have intense partisanship superintended by partisan horizons.

Nietzsche is not much worried about zealotry; his main worry is about apathy. A proponent of moderation, who does worry about zealotry, might counsel against unconditional aspirations per se; wisdom prohibits totalistic dedications in favor of qualified ones, because it is dangerous, as well as unrealistic, to suppose that anything is all-important. I have covered this ground in various contexts; suffice it to say here that where conduct is concerned we have much reason to be skeptical of the absolute, but a categorical ban on unconditional commitment would also be unrealistic and might even be considered immoderate.[14]

If we have to acknowledge, with Nietzsche, that any vigorous action in the affairs of the world depends upon some perspective or other, and therefore has the character of one-sidedness, the basic question is whether the limited horizons under which we act are at all subject to a reasonably philosophic judgment that is independent of them. In other words, can anyone ever plausibly judge that some worldviews are better than others? Here is a possible test: horizons can be broader or narrower, so you can try to judge on the basis of breadth; "all men are created equal" is more cosmopolitan than "my country [or my group] right or wrong." While this way of thinking about it can be helpful, it cannot be conclusive; Nietzsche would say that this is evaluation in the service of a democratic bias that is finally indefensible. Insofar as Nietzsche evaluates, it is on the basis of what most powerfully energizes. We can counter with horrible examples: the Nazis and the Communists have had horizons that energized them quite a bit; so do the radical Islamists. The first two are almost universally condemned now as wrong, and not simply on account of the fact that they were militarily and politically defeated. Horrible examples may be helpful, but they can be intellectually compelling only insofar as one can have access to an understanding of humanity that is not simply perspectival in the Nietzschean sense. Then one could argue that the Nazis were wrong in their claim that some races or ethnicities are subhuman, and that the Communists were wrong in their premise that human individuals are susceptible of thoroughgoing collectivization, and that we flourish thereby. As for the radical Islamists, we can argue forcefully that, at minimum, what people want—and want reasonably—is that they and their loved ones shall remain securely alive, and that to slaughter or subjugate those you choose to label as infidels is an enterprise destructive of all prospects for civilized existence. (It is no derogation of the argument that it cannot be made *to them* for they do not listen.) Do these and the like evaluations merely reflect the limited and biased horizons of John Locke or of modern Western liberalism? It seems to me that the burden of proof rests upon those who would insist that these amount to no more than liberal prejudice. It is hardly a mere parochial prejudice that a respect for human life and for individual personality is the necessary precondition for the maintenance of any civilized culture.

Nietzscheans might insist upon hearing what we mean by "civilized" and why one should prefer that condition to its alternatives. The idea at its political root envisions a basic rule of law with these two defining imperatives: That, to the greatest extent possible, violence among society's members is to be precluded and everyone's life and means of life are to be protected, *and* that governing policies are to be legislated or deliberately enacted in the form of general rules applicable to everyone and knowable in advance of their application. Among other things, the rule of law allows for a rational human existence as the alternatives to it do not. Where life itself isn't constantly threatened, where self-preservation isn't your perpetually overwhelming concern, then there is a possibility of devoting your attention to higher cultural pursuits. When you know in advance what the rules are, and hence the limits within which others are likely to behave, then you are much freer to think in a deliberative way about life plans than you would be in the absence of such rules where anything can happen anytime.[15] From this foundation advanced arts and sciences can develop, and from the influence of arts and sciences upon minds, personalities emerge that are, in one degree or another, self-reflective and reflective in relations with each other. When someone is said to be a very civilized or civil person, you expect to encounter a person whose elementary passions have undergone refinement, who thinks before he or she acts, and who is likely to treat you and your ideas with the measure of respect we call "civility." We could say that civilization originates with the establishment of law and order and proceeds, at its best, to facilitate cultivation of a certain kind of mind that is the opposite of barbaric. Why are these conditions valuable and preferable? The case for them need not rest simply on the fact that almost all of us (not only the "last men") want very much to stay alive but also and ultimately on the argument that rationality, or enlightened deliberation, is an essential component of what it means to be human. Of course, this thumbnail sketch of what makes civilized life worthy neglects the problems of civilization, its discontents, and the complaints Nietzscheans would make against it. But Nietzsche's philosophy (like anyone else's) depends upon it; a barbaric culture could not produce a Nietzsche any more than it could a Socrates.[16]

Civilization supposes that enlightenment is both desirable and possible. As to the possibility, a basic issue with postmodernism is whether or not there can be such a thing as philosophic enlightenment—a genuinely contemplative truth-seeking orientation toward the condition of our species. Of course, the mind could not perform that function if its operations were always in the service and under the command of a drive for personal or group mastery. We might as well acknowledge that our thinking is frequently in this condition, and not only the thinking of the most power-hungry among us. Often enough in ordinary affairs, we calculate under the influence of pride, vanity, a craving for preeminence. We didn't need postmodernists to tell us this; seventeenth-century British philosopher Thomas Hobbes emphasized it, and Plato knew it.[17] Furthermore, one who writes books about human affairs and is self-reflective about it may recognize that among his or her motivations is a desire for control, an impetus to impose a meaningful order of one's own upon unruly events. We have to concede this much to Nietzsche: there is a creative element in large-scale intellectual endeavors that owes something to a longing for mastery.

What we need not concede, however, is that this impulse is always in the driver's seat and that the mind cannot rise above it and reflect critically upon it. We can, and sometimes do, reason about power and the claim that reasoning is always its servant; those who adamantly deny that this capability exists will eventually be found in self-contradiction if their denial takes the form of arguments for which they make truth claims. The postmodernist assault upon the very possibility of disinterested thought amounts to an assertion that is not coherently arguable. Should a postmodernist wish to reply, "So what? We don't care about coherence or about the true and the false," let us allow him or her that assertion.

Cultural relativism and postmodernism have too many problems of their own to qualify them as formidable intellectual adversaries and effective debunkers of the case for moderation. Undeniably, the understandings of human nature and its vicissitudes that have led Aristotle and others to emphasize moderation are not absolutely complete and demonstrable verities about everything of importance. That is why we have much to learn about the human condition from different philosophers and from modern psychologists, and that will always be the case. We are creatures of remarkable intricacy, with goods diverse and capabilities sometimes mysterious; the understanding of us is never complete, and propositions about us rarely lend themselves to conclusive uncontestable proofs. The enterprise is not at all like that of putting together a large puzzle, step-by-step, and generation by generation, until someday it is all finished. But if, with regard to the things most interesting to us, uncontestable demonstration is unavailable, that doesn't mean that no thinker can have access to any realities concerning the kind of being that is human; still available to us are persuasive inquiries and analyses.[18] Likewise, that the goods or desiderata we pursue are various, even diverse, hardly compels the (rather strange) conclusion that nothing may be deemed good or bad, desirable or undesirable, for humanity per se. Indeed, as we've seen, diversity is one of the factors impelling us to consider the general value of moderation. There is an understanding of the importance of moderation (of which I have sought periodically to make use) that deserves to be called classical, because it has held up rather well over time; its presence is notable among inquiries philosophic, ethical, and political in virtually every historic period; it comes back and keeps coming back.[19] That doesn't prove the case, but doesn't it, at least, get your attention?

This defense of reason and its contribution to moderation is necessarily incomplete; it can be made somewhat more complete, however, by taking account of a kind of attack upon rationality that differs from the Nietzschean attack. Irrationalist viewpoints we've considered thus far denigrate reason because they see it as a force that suppresses or undermines passion. But it is criticized from quite another angle as a prime agent in the inflammation of passions, including deleterious ones.

This critique does not (or need not) deny that rationality is the distinctively human quality, that what distinguishes us from other animals is our possession of speech, which produces abstract ideas. But, the critique contends, this is also problematic; abstract ideation gives rise to a far-reaching imagination that creates artificial desires and wants extending well beyond our natural inclinations—impetuous passions and luxurious wants owing much more to our rational than to our animal nature. Sensual desires are inflamed into imperative lusts by imagination-inspired notions and expectations of gratification rather more likely to be frustrated than satisfied. Moreover, thought makes possible egoism, pride, and vanity; it renders us self-conscious beings who acquire the need for self-esteem and disposition to demand recognition from others, with resulting inner tensions and outer conflicts. Hence reason, with its concomitant self-consciousness, is no unmitigated good; at best it is a mixed blessing.

I have just summarized a portion of the Rousseauian perspective. Rousseau says that while our passions originate in our needs, "their progress depends on that of our knowledge." Our most intense appetites and fears are the effects of thoughts, "for we cannot desire or fear anything except from the idea we have of it or from the simple impulsion of nature."[20] The impulses of nature, or in the original "state of nature," are simple and nonluxurious: preservation, not power; food, not delicacies, sex, not romance and adoration. The lusts we experience for power, luxuries, and adoration are artificial wants generated by ideas that are acquired in society and come to be felt as urgent needs. Our inflated desires become especially injurious when exacerbated by pride or vanity, and "it is reason that engenders vanity and reflection that fortifies it."[21]

Does this Rousseauian perspective contribute to the understanding of our condition, and if so, does it damage the case for moderation? Surely this much is to be said for it: abstract ideation does indeed complicate and often inflame our affects, making it possible for us to entertain dangerously utopian expectations, distort reality, and even deceive ourselves. (An entire school of contemporary psychiatry, cognitive therapy, treats neurotic malaise as a consequence of false perceptions or exaggerated cognition.)[22] But this wreckage hardly tells the whole story about the effects of reason in our lives; mustn't we also consider how reason serves to overcome dangerous delusions and modify imaginary expectations? (Every psychotherapy depends, more or less, upon a promotion of self-awareness.) Reason, in the traditional view of it anyway, is not only a certain capacity for abstract conceptualization; it is also an ability to use such capacity to see things, including who and where we are and why we do what we do. Without thought, "know thyself" is impossible, and it is even quite doubtful that without thought you could come to have a self at all. Rousseau is right that reason engenders vanity, in the sense that a creature lacking any traces of the former is lacking any potentiality for the latter; Rousseau's original man has no ego about which to be egotistic. Who among us would want to trade places with that "man" and pay that price?

The "natural man"—solitary, simple, and nonaggressive—is, as our author acknowledges, a hypothetical construct meant to be illuminating for certain purposes. That person is in no need of faculties for self-control; he is spontaneously temperate. But Rousseau is at pains to sketch out a long historical process by which we have become something else: creatures full of demanding passions and ambitions, divided within ourselves and often dangerous. This might not get us all the way to Freudian man, but it comes close to a picture of that human nature for which classical thought strongly recommends a disciplinary moderation. In that regard it matters little through what evolutionary process, if any, we came to be this way. Rousseau does not deny the importance of self-controlling character and social constraints for the kind of beings men and women now are and who have to live together in civilization. Though he seems to deem it optimal if you could, in some sense, "go back to nature," Rousseau regards that as an impossibility for the great mass of us who must try to make do with what help we can get from reasoning and civil norms.

I suggest that Rousseau is not the enemy of moderation that he is thought to be by some critics—and by some devotees or quasi-devotees who are disposed to make war on all social establishments and civic authority on behalf of the spontaneous life. Yet we cannot leave it at that, because some of his writings offer a conception of the subject distinguishable in an interesting way from the traditional one. Consider this from his *Emile*:

> What is the cause of man's weakness? It is found in the disproportion between his strengths and his needs. It is our passions that make us weak, for our natural strength is not enough for their satisfaction. To limit our desires comes to the same thing as to increase our strength.[23]

The point Rousseau makes here, and much emphasizes, is offered as the crux of a definition of freedom and indeed of happiness, but it also lends itself to an inquiry about moderation. If you want really to be free, make sure that your desires are in proportion to your capabilities such that you can satisfy them by your own independent effort; in other words, avoid desires which are excessive in the sense that they exceed your capacity. Aristotelians could agree with this proposition in large part, while countering that, since people are social beings, one is very unlikely to be able to confine his or her wants to those satisfiable independently. More to our point, the idea of moderation suggested by Rousseau is less focused upon self-restraint than it is upon not having or acquiring the passions that would require substantial restraint and discipline. This desideratum reminds us of Rousseau's original man, who is free from imperious passions and from burdens imposed by a far-reaching imagination. Perhaps we should regard this Rousseauian concept as an ideal model meant to guide our thinking about what would be optimal if you could get it, and thereby to encourage some efforts at approximation to it in some favorable situations. (Live the simple life, as simple as possible; try to reside and bring up your children far from cities and the corrupting influences thereof.)[24] At any rate, Rousseauian thought adds a dimension to our inquiry about what moderation involves. In theory at least, there are two ways of being moderate: one controls certain strong passions, or one contrives to avoid infection by them in the first place; self-discipline or simplicity of life. Or both. Rousseau regards the latter as closer to the ideal but allows for the former because, in agreement with the classical tradition, he takes seriously the pervasiveness among us of deleterious affects.

I hope no one can conclude from the rationale for moderation presented in these chapters that it takes a dismally pessimistic view of human nature. The view taken is not that we are bad but that we are mixed (often mixed up); we have within us some urges demanding and self-centered that are deleterious when uncontained, but we also have capabilities to employ means, including communal means, to contain them. Plato's Socrates observes rather soberly that there are wild and brutish desires that "probably come to be in everyone; but when checked by the laws and the better desires, with the help of argument, in some human beings they are entirely gotten rid of or only a few weak ones are left, while in others stronger and more numerous ones remain."[25] This Socratic pronouncement is neither very optimistic nor very pessimistic about our prospects. It is nuanced: some of us will fare better than others with the Dionysian element of our existence. But, overall, that element is said to be tolerably manageable with human resources—communities, with the laws and norms they establish, and our better inclinations aided by "argument," that is, reasonable speech.

The book of Genesis disagrees; it teaches that resources merely human are manifestly inadequate and moreover troublesome. After all, Adam and Eve were ejected from the Garden of Eden for (disobediently) tasting that apple of knowledge. An inference one may draw from the Garden of Eden story is that our possession of knowledge is something problematic for us. The first reported consequence of its acquisition is that they were aware and ashamed of their nakedness; self-consciousness, which they now have, makes it possible to feel shame and indeed makes that likely. The last consequence revealed to them before their expulsion is that they will die: "You are dust and to dust you shall return." If the story is read as part of an account of the human condition, we see that reason brings with it the awareness of death. We also witness in the expulsion an alienation from pristine nature to which creatures having become self-conscious can no longer be related in spontaneous harmony and serenity.

Like the Rousseauian men who have left the state of nature, the men who appear after Eden are beset with overriding passions, anxieties, and vices.[26] The vices that appear after Eden are of two different sorts: arrogant self-importance or pride, and grossly inflated sensuality or beastliness. The former is epitomized in the story of Babel wherein men presumptuously assert self-sufficiency: "Come let us build ourselves a city and a tower with its top in the heavens and let us make a name for ourselves."[27] The latter is epitomized in the lusts and violence of Sodom and Gomorrah. Only reasoning creatures or sophisticated minds could have built that tower and entertained the vainglorious ambition to define themselves ("make a name for ourselves") and do so independently of the Deity, and the citizens of Sodom and Gomorrah are possessed by domineering lusts or bloated hedonism that could not have been felt by the simple and unaware inhabitants of Eden. The message is that the capabilities acquired by post-Edenic man render him susceptible of two persistent temptations: we can try to act as if we were gods, and we can try to act as if we were only sophisticated animals preoccupied with animal pleasures that we are able to intensify.

Yet there also appear after Eden human beings of a different sort: trustworthy men of moral stature such as Noah and Abraham. Noah is a person with whom God can make a compact. Abraham is a person who, while obedient to the Divine commands, is capable of remonstrating with God about God's apparent decision to destroy everyone in Sodom and Gomorrah.[28] These men have the character and ability to lead a people on the torturous path that Genesis depicts. The knowledge of good and evil acquired through the fall produces creatures much worse than Adam and some who rise to a stature well above that of Adam. Knowledge accompanied by self-awareness is not, according to Genesis, simply an evil; it is a mixed or ambiguous benefit with some promising potentialities. Consequent to it our horizons are broadened–for good and ill.

Reason is a beneficent power when subordinate to and under the direction of God; it is reason's claim to self-sufficiency that is wrong and the source of wrongs. In other words, our intelligence becomes threatening when it has no limits, when it has nothing to look up to for guidance and constraint.[29] Can a nontheistic classical philosophy answer this "argument" of Genesis? There is a sense in which it cannot; reflection, however enlightened, is in no position to refute the claim that the Divinity—a divinity of the sort the Bible envisions—exists. The counterargument, if we should call it that, would have to take the form of showing that reason, at its best, is able to recognize its own limits—that it can be self-questioning and perceptive of the great probability that not everything is knowable. Moral philosophy is supposed to be soberly concerned with what is and isn't good for such beings as we are; an enlightened reflection on that subject should be able to discern that a boundless hubristic rationalism is not good for us. (Even Nietzsche's nonsober reflection weighs in against it.) In defense of Socratic thinking we may affirm that reason does have something to look up to: truth, in its many-sided intricacy. If one respects the truth, awareness of its intricacies should serve as a stumbling block against hubris, even as the stimulus to a certain form of humility; there are important things regarding which Socrates "knows that he does not know." Devotion to an examined life need not be incompatible with awareness that mysteries exist; indeed it can be an avenue to their discovery.

Why should one be devoted to an examined life? This ultimate question can be raised from a skeptical viewpoint as well as from a religious viewpoint. Aristotle says that "all men desire to know," but many of us apparently desire other things more. There is a utilitarian answer to the question: you will have irresolvable practical problems otherwise. A more impressive, nonutilitarian philosophic answer would take a long time to elaborate, but thinking about it can be facilitated by observation of what goes on in Platonic dialogues among the more and the less ignorant.

Classical thought and Genesis have at least one theme in common: the teaching that human nature is composite, that man is a divided being possessing recalcitrant inclinations requiring moral regulation. Genesis gives us two different stories of the creation of mankind which precede the fall; in chapter 1 "God created man in His own image," and in chapter 2 "the Lord formed men of dust from the ground." Somehow we are likenesses of God *and* we are made out of dust—something both material and transient; from the beginning the human being is constituted by a duality, the effects of which one sees pervasively played out in the Hebrew Bible. While the divine aspect can raise our sights, the material side binds us to earthy needs and wants that knowledge, when it comes, can inflame. This view of our basic condition is both similar to and different from the classical duality of reasonable speech and the irrational (inflatable by unreasonable speech). What they fundamentally agree about is that there is hierarchy among the soul's components; we have within us a higher and a lower element, and dealing with the lower is both imperative and fraught with difficulties.

At sharp variance with both of these orientations is the postmodernist dream of limitless personal freedom in a world without authoritative norms, and in which nothing is "higher" or "lower," a dream prefigured in certain modern liberal doctrines that portray (or presuppose) as the optimal human being the autonomous individual who freely chooses his or her own "lifestyle," even his or her own "identity." Let us call this outlook, which features personal choice as the desideratum above all desiderata, autonomism. From this vantage point, what classical and biblical ethics have most deeply in common is the rejection of autonomism as an immoderate aspiration, unrealistic and not good for us.

What of the dustlike transience of our existence and our awareness of inevitable death? Does a case for moderation not theologically inspired lose its strength when that awesome fact comes clearly to mind? Religious faiths answer to our fear of death; can "argument" have anything to say about it?

Among the tribulations we undergo from anxiety about death are various forms of immoderation. At one extremity, aspirations can be undermined and vitality lost when the fear pervades one's attitudes and overcomes one's other affects; at the alternative extreme, passions can be grossly intensified as efforts to suppress, counteract, or deny the cognizance of inevitable nonbeing. As to the latter, you might seek distraction through some frenetic addiction or other, including a certain kind of addiction to incessant sexuality, whereby you manage to be oblivious—for a time—to the terrible fact of mortality. To continue this line of speculation, a lust for power or domination might be, at bottom, driven by an urge, subconscious though compelling, to deny that one is a fragile creature destined soon enough for the dust. Conquest, political or sexual, appears to function for some persons, self-deceptively no doubt, as an antidote to the fragility and transience of existence. The same might be said about the glory-seeking man whose desire is to be remembered in renown, if not eternally then for a long, long time; fame can be envisioned as a form of immortality. (One of the messages receivable from the Tower of Babel is that its architects are emphatically asserting that they are by no means dust; perhaps Alexander the Great was activated by such a motive, which didn't save him from dying at the age of thirty-three.)

Apparently the inexorable termination of life, with our anxious cognizance of it, is not really answerable by exercises of power; on this subject even a thoroughgoing Nietzschean will to power would seem to be of no help. (So, you have been masterful; what now?) Can the inexorable reality be turned into a question answerable in some degree by rational means?

The initial practical question about death is: shall I think about it or avoid thinking about it? Montaigne, in his remarkable and much-remarked upon essay "That to Philosophize Is to Learn How to Die," opts for having death often in mind. "Let us learn to meet it steadfastly and combat it. And to begin to strip it of its greatest advantage against us, let us take an entirely different way from the usual one. Let us rid it of its stratagems, come to know it, get used to it. . . . It is uncertain where death awaits us; let us await it everywhere."[30] Frequently kept in mind, the prospect of your death loses its terrible awesomeness, becoming something familiar—a natural fact of all life, to which everyone is subject, and to which, with the appropriately thoughtful effort, you can accommodate in equanimity. Montaigne (a nominal Christian, if at all), offered as his ideal model of this thoughtful equanimity the example of Socrates, whose serenity about dying is legendary.[31] Yet, as Montaigne surely knew, Socrates was a most extraordinary person, and Socratic serenity is a rare thing. Given the vicissitudes of the project, we ordinary people may only hope, at best, to travel some distance toward the practical wisdom that Montaigne recommends.

Here is a line of argument to the effect that moderation can help. You will be better off with the mortality issue if you develop a character including habits that temper the importunities of the irrational. Raging emotions distort judgment and obstruct reflection, about death as well as other things. Of course, the relevant emotion is fear, natural and of no small proportion, but the odds are that someone habitually effective in handling emotions per se will be in better shape to manage this one. Perhaps the point is more persuasively stated in the negative: raging passions stimulate raging imagination—in this case, images of the horrible and the miserable—and these in turn (as Rousseau would remind us) exacerbate the affects. Moderation might counsel, as Montaigne does, reflection upon my inevitable demise, but it counsels much against unconstrained rumination upon its awfulness; one is almost certain to be anxious, but one doesn't have to be terrorized. The specifically relevant quality of character is, of course, courage or fortitude; as we've noted, courage in the classical and Aristotelian sense is not utter fearlessness but basically an engrained modification of primal fears so that they don't overwhelm you. And the enterprise of engraining should start early enough that the habit of facing dangers, and confidence in doing so, can become part and parcel of who you are.

There is both good and bad news here. The good news is that, through character, a person can have some control over the extent of his fears. The bad news is that you didn't have much to say about the influences attending the early stages of your character development; that was a matter of luck. (Montaigne reports that he had an excellent father.) Given the contingencies of our origins, as well as our termination, we cannot be the entire masters of our destiny; chance or fortune is manifestly in power at the beginning and at the end of a life (often enough in other parts of it too). But the notion sometimes entertained that, on this account, a self-controlling character is impossible or unimportant is a standing invitation to immoderation and its consequences.[32]

Any general account of moderation and the rationale for it necessarily depends upon some generalizations about human beings and the desirable and the undesirable. I have responded to the most radical forms of (contemporary) denial that such generalization can be credible, but there is a less radical way of being skeptical about generality. In this regard Montaigne's writings are instructive. Here is an observation he makes over and over again: "Truly man is a marvelously vain, diverse and undulating object. It is hard to found any consistent and uniform judgment on him."[33] Prior to the twentieth century, Montaigne was the secular philosopher most devoted to emphasizing human variability and inconstancy—how much we contradict ourselves, and how often supposed truths about us are contradicted by counterexamples. His work and his brand of skepticism stand as a formidable obstacle to the kind of universalistic theorizing that would purport to define exactly the basic human goods and systematically formulate the priorities among them.[34] Yet, though precluding the doctrinaire, Montaigne manages to offer general observations and insights about the way we are and about better and worse; his reflections would be of considerably less interest to us if he only spoke of particulars. Moreover, Montaigne is a self-proclaimed moderate who can be found, periodically in the *Essays*, recommending moderation—not only with a view to his own unique situation, but also as a way of life appropriate for his readers.

Montaigne, like all interesting moral psychologists, meditates upon what is and isn't conducive to well-being. In a striking example concerning his special interest in the desideratum of personal independence, he writes, "We should have wife, children, goods, and above all health, if we can; but we must not bind ourselves to them so strongly that our happiness depends on them. We must reserve a backshop all our own, entirely free, in which to establish our real liberty and our principle interest and solitude."[35] He concludes that "the greatest thing in the world is to know how to belong to oneself."[36] You could tax Montaigne with the epistemological question, "How do you know that this is such a great thing or any good thing at all?" A preliminary and nonscientific answer comes to mind. This desideratum strongly appeals to us, doesn't it? So, reflect upon that appeal and the sources of it. Consult your experience and that of others about the conditions and vicissitudes of happiness. Let us not tax Montaigne too much with theoretical questions of that sort, and let us set aside the theoretical question I've raised about "self" (what is it?). In Montaigne's practical view, a large part of what belonging to oneself means is that you do not give yourself entirely to anyone or anything else; you may have family, loved ones, and a country, but never allow these attachments to sink so deep that they constitute your identity. Another large part is moderation; the tempering of wants and expectations is an indispensable means to the end, for intense passions and grand expectations have the effect of placing our happiness at the mercy of others whom we will need to get these satisfied, and at the mercy of fortuitous external events. "But the passions that distract me from myself and attach me elsewhere, those in truth I oppose with all my strength."[37] This seems to mean that I should love others always with reservation and only myself unconditionally. And this, I think, is the question most worth pursuing.

Montaigne's position could be charged with a kind of extremism: moderation in the service ultimately of a resolute self-centeredness. A more balanced view is suggested in the old rabbinical saying: "If I am not for myself who will be for me, and if I am only for myself what am I?" Man is, after all, both an individual and a social being, subject to imperatives from both directions. But the rabbis, and those of us who appreciate their formulation, cannot just leave it at that level of abstraction. What about situations in which the two imperatives diverge, even conflict; when the chips are down, where are the priorities? Montaigne opts for the priority of one's individuality, on the basis of an insight about well-being; for him "nature" so dictates. Man is a highly variable creature but not infinitely so: by nature, our underlying care and concern is for ourselves.

On my reading, Montaigne, despite his debunking of universals, affirms a preeminent human good: self-possession or, more exactly, self-possession in tranquility, and moderation of our wants is its minister.[38] This outlook is distinguishable from a boundless autonomism that celebrates liberation from all restraints so everyone can act just as they please. (The claim about the primacy of belonging to oneself is made in an essay entitled "Of Solitude"; it is about preservation of an inner life.) And Montaigne's idea is a far cry from "the will to power" and the agitated vitalism of some Romantics, allowing, as they do not, a major role for a tempering practical reasonableness in successful human living. Reflective minds should be able to see why there is much to be said for this. So too, however, is there much to be said for the rabbinical tradition, which apparently strikes a different balance between our individuality and our sociality. But these two outlooks are not, in respects relevant to the importance of moderation, stark opposites. They both affirm that self-love is a good and self-discipline a necessity.

Yet what finally should we think of Montaigne's central idea that self-possession is the chief good, and the corollary that, in its interest, wisdom dictates avoidance of unconditional attachments to others? It seems to me that an inner life wherein one belongs to oneself is an important human good but isn't the ultimately exclusive good that Montaigne's corollary suggests. Perhaps a philosophy of moderation can serve to reduce the distance between belonging to oneself and commitment to others by calling attention to a connection between them. Human beings are not simply independent individuals who engage in instrumental relations with each other; our personal identities are shaped and enlarged by social connections, especially with those we love or admire, and we are in need of that love and admiration, aren't we? You need to be "for others"; without social bonds and loyalties beyond the self, your horizons would be so narrow that you could hardly be said to have much of a self to possess. Yet the opposite condition would lead to a similarly undesirable result; one wholly possessed and entirely constituted by relations with others and the neediness thereof could hardly be considered to have free agency and a life of one's own. No general theory of the good life can prescribe for all of us exactly how to navigate between the precipices of a solipsistic individualism at one extremity and, at the other, no individuality—though moral philosophy can show us that these *are* precipices, each one involving the sacrifice of something crucial to our humanity. Of course, a radical skeptic may continue to maintain that none of this is persuasive, because, really, there is no "humanity"; but let such a skeptic bear the appropriately heavy burden of argument.

Among the various sets of precipices to which I've alluded in these essays, there is one calling for reconsideration as we conclude, and that is the pervasive problem of pride. Quite apparently we are beings who are not only capable of having an opinion of ourselves but who can scarcely avoid it, and we seek the admiration of others in order to think well of ourselves. It is perhaps an embarrassment to consider how much of human action and rumination is attributable to the desire for recognition; undeniably some persistent human nature is at work here.

The problem in its most elementary form is about self-esteem; to what extent should I think well of myself? Nowadays self-esteem is strongly recommended, especially in educational circles, as a psychological necessity and an imperative precondition for achievement; you've just got to have it (and your mentors had better strive to promote it). But isn't there such a thing as too much of it? A bloated, grandiose opinion of myself—my virtues and what is due to me from others—is appropriately called vanity, and in the most extreme cases is recognized as pathology. At the other extremity is self-contempt, or lack of self-respect, a debilitating condition that sends many to psychiatric or other counseling. We can easily see how narcissism, an exaggerated self-importance, often obstructs one's ability to confront realities, as does self-denigration with the disabilities it engenders; the ego-inflated person cannot recognize his or her limits and the self-deprecator his or her possibilities. The deleterious consequences of these conditions manifestly extend beyond the individuals infected by them; you may seek power over others to feed an inflated ego or to compensate a deflated one. What person who has thought about the matter can fail to perceive the advisability of a middle way that somehow manages to combine self-respect and a measure of humility?[39]

Where is the middle ground? An Aristotelian outlook would counsel (as does the Socratic model) that you should soberly assess your merits and have as much pride as is warranted by them, but no more. No doubt this is easier said than done. The Gospels counsel humility, which, according to reflective interpretation, does not mean self-contempt but an authentic acknowledgment of one's inevitably great weaknesses, with consequent sympathy for the weaknesses of others and openness to God's help. This too is easier said than done. But with regard to how, ideally, one ought to judge oneself, those, it seems to me, are the grand alternatives. Can they be combined; can we take some of each? No and yes. In one sense, of course, we cannot; these alternatives arise from diverse worldviews, the former oriented to our deliberative faculty and the latter to faith. The tensions between these grand horizons, while amenable to thought, are not removable by thought. In another sense, however, we can learn from each about vicissitudes of being human; each reveals and explores pervasive human deficiencies and causes thereof, and neither will countenance hubris, so often rooted in the proud claim that I am or can be the entire master of my destiny. Yet neither teaching will countenance a hopelessness or utter pessimism about our prospects.

The middle ground between too much pride and too little is occupied by a mind that is able to acknowledge limitations and possibilities, thereby including requisites of humility and requisites of self-confidence. An important ingredient of humility is the recognition and acceptance of contingency and uncertainty, acknowledgment that, inescapably, factors—inner as well as outer, of which we cannot be in command—set outer limits to what one can do and be. An important ingredient of self-respect is that you recognize, and act upon the recognition, that within these outer limits you can be, with effort, a self-controlling, hence self-directing agent. Those of us who think far too well of ourselves or far too

112 / On Moderation

little have one failing in common: we lack perspective—not as Nietzsche employed the term, but as it is used in the commonplace expression, "Don't get so absorbed in something that you lose perspective"—that is, awareness of the larger human or moral context and consequently a sense of proportion.

Most broadly considered, moderation has two aspects: it is an outlook, a way of viewing realities, and it is a state of character. The qualities these two aspects encompass do not come to be in us spontaneously; they are capabilities attainable in gradations and always by effort. Why make the effort; why should one want the ensemble of qualities called moderation? The kind of answer to which much of these inquiries has pointed is that it is an antidote or alternative to a number of things we don't want. Stated in positive terms, it is requisite for many things we do want considerably: thoughtfulness, friendship and other mutualities, enduring love, tranquility or order in our lives insofar as we can get it, and self-possession to the extent that we can achieve it. Who could deny that these are goods that constitute happiness, whether or not reason could manage any general ranking of their relative importance? This kind of answer suggests that moderation is always and only instrumental—a means to other ends, as distinguished from an end desirable in itself. Yet there is another way of conceptualizing the subject, which I hope this inquiry has also suggested; with regard to some of these goods, we can consider moderation not only as a means but also as a desideratum belonging to the end. It is, arguably, not only a precondition for friendship but an intrinsic component of a genuine friendship.[40] And that inner tranquility which is inseparable from self-possession is also inseparable from moderation.

Conclusion

I do not suppose that this inquiry has resolved all questions. Here I will revisit, briefly, a few of the points I've been most interested in making—with a view to entertaining some critical questions you might still want to raise.

Chapter 1 explored consequences of the important reality that "you cannot get it all" from any social arrangements, no matter how well conceived. Hence, statesmanship must weigh and balance inevitably competing goods and interests, with the result that, in one degree or another, concessions are made and compromises achieved. This reality can be denied or obfuscated in two ways; that is, in this regard there are two modes of extremism. I could insist upon maximizing one good (individual rights or civic order, for example), because I refuse to recognize that significant desiderata are at variance with my desideratum; this is absolutism. Or I could naively suppose that we *can* get it all, and that only on account of very unjust institutions and exploitive persons we don't have a society fulfilling our every moral aspiration; this is utopianism. Absolutism and utopianism are fertile sources for a politics of righteous rage. But aren't we entitled, even obliged, to be angry about some political situations? Yes, but not on absolutist or utopian grounds.

Political moderation is sometimes identified with lack of principled conviction. That is inaccurate; you can, and should, have more than one principle. You might want to call attention to occasions where one precept clearly ought to take precedence over others. But in these cases, prudence usually dictates that the others be kept in view as limiting or qualifying factors. For example, the freedom to assemble and demonstrate collectively in protest of public policies is central in a liberal democracy, but public tranquility and private property rights are not to be forgotten (demonstrations *how* and *where?*). Another example comes from the currently agitated issue of national security and civil liberties. The kind of mentality I'm calling moderation will always consider both of these vital imperatives, though it will also be much aware of critical circumstances bearing upon them. This mentality is able to acknowledge circumstances dictating the priority of national security, but when doing so it will continue to take account of the civil liberties side of the equation. A final illustration: in a democracy, claims made on behalf of civic equality are frequently entitled to trump competing claims. But the following is too much trumping: during the French Revolution, radicals marched in the streets proclaiming, "We will have equality or we will destroy civilization." They meant total substantive equality right now.

A critic of my rationale for moderation might offer this challenge: "What you advance as a case for moderation is really a case for conservatism. Its emphasis on the dangers of political idealism counsels a readiness to accept many social imperfections, even sizeable ones, and, by implication at least, a disposition in favor of traditionally hallowed institutions and ways of doing things. That is conservative." This claim is worth consideration. In some respects the line of argument in my first chapter does point in a conservative direction. While allowing for reformist politics, it takes a dim view of transformationism and stresses limitations rooted in our human and social condition. And, as the critic would be anxious to observe, the conservative position is problematic, insofar as history shows us how highly valued alterations in our social condition have been inspired by single-minded absolutists who turned a blind eye to considerations in competition with their cherished ideal. One answer is that at least as often the absolutist posture has wreaked havoc, and its usual tendency is to render desirable compromise impossible. But I would rather call attention to respects in which the position taken in these essays may point in a liberal direction. As frequently indicated, a significant element in moderate leadership is its nondogmatic character; the leader is aware of the fact that there exists a plurality of goods to be sought and evils to be avoided. This awareness of different perspectives for which legitimacy may be claimed is a kind of open-mindedness, and open-mindedness is a liberal virtue; at least it is a virtue extolled in historic Western liberalism. Open-mindedness has its problems, which I've noted from time to time, and of which Nietzsche is the most powerful expositor, but does my critic want to say that its problem is a bias in favor of conservatism? Here is another way to put it: among the most prominent themes in this book is that of the distancing function as a key component of moderation. Is a capacity to distance oneself from partisan demands and pressing passions of the moment a conservative capacity more than a liberal one? This is, after all, a capacity featured in liberal education and by educators ranging from Socrates to Robert Maynard Hutchins.

The line of inquiry this book has pursued entails the proposition that there is such a thing as a centrist orientation transcending the distinction ordinarily made between liberal and conservative. Gilbert and Sullivan proclaim that "every child who is born alive / is either a little liberal or a little conservative," but Gilbert and Sullivan were making a joke. A theory of moderation must argue for the availability of a more comprehensive horizon beyond the opinions or values in contention here and now, an orientation toward civic (and other) well-being that enables judgment about the contending partisanships.

Yet a case for the virtue of political moderation should avoid contradicting itself by making excessive claims for this virtue. However broadly defined, the concept has its limits. Moderation, even at its best, does not provide all the qualities required of public leadership; it is, for example, no guarantor of decisiveness, which can be every bit as important. Indeed, at times of major emergency, decisiveness is often what counts the most, and this even at some risk of immoderation. Politics is an arena of contingencies.[1]

Outer limits to the virtue of moderation also appear in our personal lives and interpersonal relations. Romantic love, with the emotive vitality so central to it, presents us with a paradigmatic illustration: the arena of love is where the adage "moderation in all things" would seem to encounter its greatest or most obvious limitations, which is why I have devoted so much attention to the subject.

Shakespeare's Hamlet pays tribute to moderation when he credits his friend Horatio for not being "passion's slave." But in the grip of romantic love, aren't you necessarily and desirably passion's slave? Chapter 2 argues at length why you had better not be entirely such, yet the chapter fully acknowledges that the virtue of moderation can claim little credit for that ardent affection which so many of us (moderates included) cherish so much. (And one who would subject his ardent affection to a rigorous cost-benefit analysis is no lover.) However, I have concluded that, insofar as love is a mutual identification among two personalities meant to be lasting, the mind is necessarily involved, and one thing that minds are designed to do is make judgments. A judgment you are well advised to make, as best you can, is about the moral character of the person you are falling in love with, and the ability to do that depends upon character.

The central theme of my second chapter is that of moral character as indispensable mediator between thought and passion ("moral" understood in its broad classical sense and "character" understood primarily as engrained habituation that serves to temper or sublimate the irrational). In recent modernity, character has become a contested concept in need of defense against outlooks adversarial to it.

The simplest way to depict the adversarial outlooks is to say that, regarding what makes for successful living, they opt against a self-restraining character in favor of a vitally self-expressive or self-assertive personality. This simple formulation has to be elaborated, and, so as not to be unduly repetitious, I will reformulate the elaborations previously provided.

According to existential and some forms of romantic thought, the most important thing in the world is to be "authentic," and the worst thing is to be inauthentic. Authenticity is not easy to define; for a synonym my dictionary gives us "genuine"; it is the opposite of whatever is artificial, counterfeit, or insincere. Philosophically, the origins of the idea that genuineness is the essence of a good or worthy human life can be found in Rousseau. Civilization, Rousseau taught, imposes artificial norms and expectations that turn us into artificial beings alienated from our natural existence; the optimal condition, if you could manage it, would be to recover, beneath those layers of conventionality, the spontaneous promptings of your own nature. In other words, the genuine man gets "the feeling of his existence" from the inside, not the outside.

The interesting question confronting proponents of authenticity is what exactly is to be found inside. For Rousseau, it is an elementary and nonaggressive feeling of one's existence. For later Romantics, it is a grand passion. For Nietzsche, it is the will to power—a will to creative overcoming and predominance. For Sartre, it is a resolute volition that defines the self in perpetual rebellion against the deceptive placidity of ordinary life, especially ordinary bourgeois life. While these options can point you in different directions, none points in the direction of the balanced, self-moderating character as a crucial desideratum.

If we think of authenticity in the more familiar sense, spontaneity and the avoidance of pretense come to mind; it is unworthy to pretend to be what you are not. In classical thought, there is ample room for the injunction against pretense. At the conclusion of Plato's *Apology*, Socrates urges his friends to supervise his sons as follows: "If they seem to you to care for riches or for any other thing more than excellence, and if they think that they are something when they are really nothing, reproach them, as I have reproached you, for not caring for what they should and for thinking that they are something when really they are nothing."[2] We find two principles here, and neither is about utter spontaneity or acting only in accordance with what you really feel. One of them is about avoiding self-inflating delusions about who you are, and the other says emphatically that, among the things one might care about, some are worthier or more valuable than others. We could say that authenticity is recognized in Socratic thought as a good, but by no means the only good.

Let us not undertake here to unravel the Socratic meaning of excellence. Yet there is a debate to be had about what is the more excellent or more admirable way to live. Proponents of moderation may assert that what counts the most is self-directing character, sobriety of judgment, and willingness to entertain differing viewpoints that naturally arise in human affairs. Some adversaries may claim that what counts more than anything is the emotive—that I act upon a passion that is really my own passion. And some adversaries may proclaim, or imply, that the supreme virtue (if they would allow it to be called a virtue) is relentless commitment—that I devote myself resolutely to an overriding purpose that is really my own purpose. If we must acknowledge that there is something to be said on all sides of such a debate, must we acknowledge that it can end only in irresolvable stalemate? I do not think so; quite arguably, the outlook I've been calling moderation can account for the importance of passion and purposefulness more than their romantic and existential devotees can account for important ingredients of moderation. One might add that self-discipline is often more impressive than self-expression, because it is more demanding; Nietzsche would accept this point. However, I would rather conclude the debate with the help of Jane Austen, who teaches us that while sense and sensibility are sometimes at variance, we need them both, and a personality can be developed that accommodates both of them.

At a more philosophic level, a large question remains concerning truth and skepticism in the rationale for moderation. You might think that my argument has gone back and forth on this question. On the one hand, a general case for moderation depends upon certain truth claims about human nature and well-being; on the other hand the argument against absolutism emphasizes limitations upon what we can reasonably hope to know about the good and the bad, the desirable and the undesirable, and that is a kind of skepticism.

From time to time one may encounter the observation that skepticism is the distinctive characteristic of a civilized person; Justice Oliver Wendell Holmes was fond of that proposition. Presumably the folks asserting that proposition do not mean to carry it so far as to debunk norms supportive of civilization against barbarism, but they do have a point. The point they have is that a mature and thoughtful person has some doubts; the fanatic has no doubts (and is therefore, by the way, utterly humorless). Presumably Justice Holmes, and those American pragmatists who have celebrated doubt the way he did, have managed, on whatever basis, to believe that fanaticism is irrational and wrong. One is hard put, however, to envision how contemporary radical relativists and postmodernists, who deny that there is any rational ground at all for ethical evaluation, could find a defensible basis for disapproving of fanaticism or even defining it. If these radical denials are to be taken seriously, or literally, their philosophic supporters are in the position—which ought to be an uncomfortable one—of being wholly incapable of defending the civilization that enables their own activity.

The real relationship between moderation and skepticism is much obscured by nihilistic doctrines that debunk reason altogether; a serious exploration of the question must leave them behind. Perhaps the most interesting model of that relationship is the Socratic one; Socratic dialogues provide us with abundant illustration of occasions where demolishing comfortably received opinion is the precondition for genuinely reflective inquiry, and of the epistemological reality that doubt is a frequent companion of authentic reasoning. It has to be admitted that relentless critical inquiry of the Socratic sort may on occasion lead to quite immoderate conclusions, which is why one might be afraid of Socrates; yet we must also recognize that a necessary ingredient of self-moderating personality is an awareness that your perspective has limitations and you might be wrong.

Apart from the rigors and dilemmas of Socratic dialectic, our experience pervasively indicates that we are beings who can question ourselves. With regard to flourishing in ordinary life, we had better be in a position to do so—at least sometimes, if not always, and with Socratic persistence. The practice of Socratic questioning always and relentlessly would pose a threat of intellectual paralysis, or of moral paralysis if it precludes the tempering habituation which is also a necessary ingredient of self-moderating personality. Is this a tepid injunction to lead the examined life—sometimes? Many of us can do no better and are well advised to settle for that; we need habits and customs, even as we need at times to be able to disengage from them. If this is paradoxical, it is, I think, paradox that we are stuck with.

As to truth and skepticism in moral philosophy, the Aristotelian account makes considerable sense. There are general truths to be discovered about good character, but they cannot tell us, directly or exactly, what to do in the diverse situations with which life presents us; ethical philosophy can help, but it cannot conclusively solve our ethical problems. Aristotle provides a valuable orientation to thinking about good and bad, an orientation that, making us skeptical of the rigidly doctrinaire, also provides a prophylactic against zealotry.

Montaigne's writings cast a lot of doubt, apparently more than Aristotle does, about our capacity to arrive at valid generalizations concerning the human condition. Montaigne zestfully provides examples contradicting the usual ideas of what is good and desirable for us. Yet he stops short of utmost relativism; his essays embody more than a few generalizations on behalf of moderation. Indeed Montaigne is as well known for his espousal of moderation as he is for espousal of skepticism, and the interesting question arising is how, or to what extent, the two are related. That is one of the reasons I chose this thinker as the final philosopher to be considered in my last chapter. I here offer a few suggestions as to how Montaigne's brand of skepticism can function as a moderator.

Insofar as fanaticism feeds on the belief that one possesses absolute truth, a philosophy persistently debunking unconditional truths can serve as prophylactic against fanaticism. Moreover, Montaigne's writings heavily emphasize the power of imagination, even fantasy, in the determination of our various attitudes and outlooks toward the world, and therefore in the determination of our aspirations. If one can see that our most intense and all-consuming passions are aspirations for objects the formation of which is shaped by imaginary visions, why not contrive to give them up or to avoid acquiring them in the first place? Why be driven by fantasies? Calm down and relax your expectations; you will be better off—that is, more tranquilly self-possessed. A skeptical outlook thus contributes to moderation by teaching us that we don't have to pursue all those things we so ardently pursue; they aren't worth it. The best course is to regulate and minimize your wants so they won't overwhelm you.

I resist the temptation to get into an extended discussion of the comparisons and contrasts to be drawn between Montaigne's case for moderation and a more Aristotelian case; at this point, a few terse remarks must suffice. Personal tranquility is not so great a desideratum in the teaching of the latter as it is in the teaching of the former, and we may wonder whether Montaigne stops short of relativism enough to allow for a sufficient defense of moderation as a universal desideratum. (Largely on account of this question, my defense relies less on Montaigne). They do agree on something fundamental: self-discipline is imperative because, ultimately, harmony in the soul is a better condition than discord in the soul, however vitalizing discord might be.

Willingness to entertain doubts is a moderating virtue when it reminds me, before I launch into some totalistic commitment, that there is more than one viewpoint or consideration to take into account. Skepticism is inconducive to moderation when it goes so far as to proclaim that viewpoints about human well-being are all equal because equally indefensible. A likely response to that idea might be, "Okay, I will act on my most intense feelings, since you have shown me that there is no valid reason in the world not to do so." Nihilism is no friend of moderation and no friend of humility.

Moderation is intertwined with humility of a sort, the kind of humility that keeps us aware of our inevitable limitations—that we are all limited beings, limited in our capacity to master the unavoidable uncertainties and contingencies of life. Most religious faiths try to promote humility, and sometimes they are successful. But, as we well know, some religious beliefs incite dangerous zealotry, including mass slaughter in service to the supposed will of God. Of course, no theorizing about moderation can have much effect on that.

You might think that these essays have inclined toward pessimism about human nature and its prospects. A rosy optimism is hardly warranted; atrocities we see committed daily have their counterparts in every historical period.[3] These atrocities are not committed by beings from another planet; they indicate what we are capable of at our worst. But I have written these essays under the influence of the following two assumptions that are not pessimistic. The subject of moderation and its vicissitudes is of intrinsic interest to inquiring minds. And inquiring minds can sometimes have an effect upon the balances we must try to arrange in our public and personal lives.

CHAPTER 1

1 Moderation in the personal side of life is the subject of a separate essay; I deal with it here only insofar as character and psyche are relevant in public affairs.

2 One impressive classical effort to engage the anomalies as such is the works of Montaigne, and he found it necessary to treat the subject in a strikingly ironic way. Note particularly Montaigne's little essay "Of Moderation."

3 On a much higher theoretical level, this is the classical Aristotelian view, to which my inquiry will come in due time.

4 In the early days of the Bolshevist regime, it was suggested that Lenin could be considered a moderate political leader because his position could be located between mere social democracy on the one side and anarchistic terrorism on the other. Most commentators nowadays and almost all [formerly Soviet-dominated] "men in the streets" think otherwise.

5 Martin Diamond, *The Revolution of Sober Expectations: Delivered at Independence Square, Philadelphia, in the House of Representatives Chamber, Congress Hall, on October 24, 1973.* Washington, DC: American Enterprise Institute, 1974

6 Karl Marx, "The Communist Manifesto," in *Karl Marx: Selected Writings*, ed. David McLean (London: Oxford University Press, 1977), 246.

7   As to the aim of the French Revolution, Edmund Burke quotes this pronouncement from one of its leaders, "changer ses idees, changer ses loix, changer ses moeurs . . . changer les hommes, changer les choses . . . tout detruire, oui tout detruire, puisque tout est a recreer." (*Reflections on the Revolution in France*, in *Two Classics of the French Revolution* [New York: Doubleday, 1989], 183).

8   The well-known Madisonian argument is outlined in *Federalist Papers* 10 and 51. I will not digress here to deal with the critical claim that a price we've paid for Madisonian moderation is ethical and civic materialism—a kind of mediocrity.

9   In his works on education, John Locke writes, "I told you before that children love liberty. . . . I now tell you that they love something more, and that is dominion: and this is the first original of most vicious habits that are ordinary and natural. This love of power and dominion shows itself very early" ("Some Thoughts Concerning Education," in *John Locke on Education*, ed. Peter Gay [New York: Teachers' College, Columbia University, 1964], 76).

10 Burke, *Reflections on the Revolution in France*, 185.

11 *The Complete Essays of Montaigne*, ed. Donald M. Frame (Stanford, Calif.: Stanford University Press, 1957), 511.

12 Nietzsche says that the man of action "forgets most things in order to do one" (*The Use and Abuse of History* [Indianapolis: Bobbs-Merrill, 1949], 9).

13 Charnwood cites Lincoln in a manner pertinent to our subject. "'The battle of freedom' [Lincoln] explains in a vehement plea for what may be called moderate as against radical policy 'is to be fought out on principle. Slavery is a violation of eternal right. We have temporized with it from the necessities of our condition'" (Lord Charnwood, *Abraham Lincoln* [Mineola, N.Y.: Dover Publications, 1997], 126). On this general theme, see also Harry V. Jaffa, *Crisis of the House Divided* (Chicago: University of Chicago Press, 1999).

14 See Charnwood, *Abraham Lincoln*, 192–95.

15 They were not opposites in the political life of Winston Churchill. In the preface to his biography of Churchill, Martin Gilbert makes two seemingly divergent observations. "It was a career often marked by controversy and dogged by antagonism, for he was always outspoken and independent . . . criticizing those whom he thought were wrong." Yet "at times of national stress, Churchill was a persistent advocate of conciliation, even of coalition; he shunned the paths of division and unnecessary confrontation" (Gilbert, *Churchill: A Life* [New York: Henry Holt, 1992], xix, xx). Churchill

like Lincoln, knew when or where to conciliate and when or where to stand firm.

16 This I believe is a teaching of Plato's *Republic*, especially book V (abolishing the private family for the sake of public spiritedness), which seeks to demonstrate dramatically what we would have to sacrifice for a wholly just society of civic-minded brothers and sisters who would never think of exploiting each other.

On the decline of the Israeli kibbutzim, a recent article notes: "Of course from its earliest days, the Kibbutzim had had to negotiate an endless chain of compromises between the stringent communistic ideals of its founders and the germ of egoism [individualism] that they could never fully eradicate" (Joshua Muravchek, "Socialism's Last Stand," *Commentary*, March 2002).

17 As to the contradiction inherent in social life, Isaiah Berlin offers this useful list: "It is a commonplace that neither political equality nor efficient organization nor social justice is compatible with more than a modicum of individual liberty and certainly not with unrestrained *laissez-faire*; that justice and generosity, public and private loyalties, the demands of genius and the claims of society can violently conflict with each other. And it is no great way from that to the generalization that not all good things are compatible" (Berlin, *Four Essays on Liberty* [London: Oxford University Press, 1969], 167). It is an open question whether all of these dichotomies are as sharp as Berlin suggests. Also needing exploration is Berlin's famous recommendation of a "pluralist" society on account of these incompatibilities.

18 Berlin, *Four Essays on Liberty*, 171. I have presented one of Berlin's lists of the perpetual rivalries.

19 Berlin, *The Crooked Timber of Humanity* (Princeton: Princeton University Press, 1990), 47.

20 Galston, *Liberal Pluralism* (Cambridge: Cambridge University Press, 2002), 37.

21 Sociologists Brigette and Peter Berger make the point: "Americans have been ready to accept [cultural] differences *as long as* and only *as long as* the different groups can plausibly be seen as sharing some common values of the society. In that case ordinary and initially prejudiced Americans are quite ready to conclude that these different people are 'really okay'" (*The War Over Family: Capturing the Middle Ground* [Garden City, N.Y.: Doubleday, 1983], 183–84).

22 William Galston devotes more attention to this consideration than do most of his brethren. Galston affirms the importance of "civic unity" but also

affirms that his liberal polity must be "parsimonious in specifying binding pubic principles." The argument seems to go back and forth between these affirmations, but the heavy emphasis is upon "maximum feasible accommodation" of diversity—cultural, ideological and moral. (*Liberal Pluralism*, 20).

23 *The Federalist* (New York: Modern Library, 1937), 227.

24 Burke, *Reflections on the Revolution in France*, 263.

25 Burke, *Reflections on the Revolution in France*, 19–20, 72–73.

26 *Nichomachean Ethics*, in *Introduction to Aristotle*, ed. Richard McKeon (New York: Modern Library, 1947), 309–10.

27 *Nichomachean Ethics*, 309–10.

28 Speaking of Edmund Burke as statesman, Winston Churchill said:

> On the one hand he is revealed as the foremost apostle of Liberty, on the other as the redoubtable champion of Authority. But a charge of inconsistency applied to this great life appears a mean and petty thing. History easily discerns . . . the immense changes in the problems he was facing which evoked from the same profound mind and sincere spirit these entirely contrary manifestations. . . . No one can read the Burke of Liberty and the Burke of Authority without feeling that here was the same man pursuing the same ends, seeking the same ideals of society and government, and defending them from assaults, now from one extreme, now from the other. (Churchill, "Consistency in Politics," In *Thoughts and Adventures*, [New York: Norton, 1990], 24).

Much politics is unjustifiably inconsistent, even chameleon-like; I've been trying to distinguish that from moderation.

As for Burke's practical politics, here are some of the things Churchill must have had in mind. The Burke of Liberty generally supported the American colonists in their controversies with the British government that culminated in the Revolutionary War, and he vigorously criticized oppressive aspects of British rule in Ireland. But the Burke of Authority vigorously attacked the French Revolution because its excessive egalitarian libertinism unleashed demands that would undermine all legitimate authority, including and especially the lawful authorities essential to the balances of free government. In the last pronouncement he makes in *Reflections on the Revolution in France*, Burke depicts himself as "one who would preserve consistency by varying his means to secure the unity of his end; and when the equipoise of the vessel in which he sails may be endangered by overloading upon one side, is desirous of carrying the small weight of his reasons to that which may preserve its equipoise" (*Reflections on the Revolution in France*, 266). Nothing chameleon-like here.

29 Aristotle, *Nichomachean Ethics*, 340.

30 Aristotle, *Nichomachean Ethics*, 389.

31 Montaigne seems to take a different view of the matter. "Aristotle says that anger sometimes serves as a weapon for virtue and valor. That is quite likely; yet those who deny it answer humorously that it is a weapon whose use is novel. For we move other weapons, this one moves us, our hand does not guide it, yet it guides our hand; it holds us, we do not hold it" (*Complete Essays of Montaigne*, 545). However, Montaigne does not advocate eradication of anger, and is sometimes found expressing it.

32 In a recent work Norma Thompson makes this perceptive observation: "To register 'the extremes' is a tried and true Greek method for activating thought and we underestimate its potential when we assign static qualities to this model. Aristotle's rightly constituted polis combines the two elements of diversity and unity" (Thompson, *The Ship of State* [New Haven: Yale University Press, 2001], 46). I would say, and Thompson probably means, that Aristotle grapples very perceptibly with problems of diversity and unity at all levels of political life.

33 If there be dissent from this proposition, dissenters should consider that it is supported by thinkers as diverse as Aristotle, Locke, Nietzsche, and Freud, though each has his own way of formulating it.

34 Harry M. Clor, *Public Morality and Liberal Society* (Notre Dame, Ind.: University of Notre Dame Press, 1996).

35 See H. L. A. Hart, *Law, Liberty, and Morality* (New York: Vintage Books, 1966), 75.

36 See John Stuart Mill, *On Liberty* (New York: Liberal Arts Press, 1956), chap. 3, and Alexis de Tocqueville, *Democracy in America*, ed. and trans. Harvey C. Mansfield and Delba Winthrop (Chicago: University of Chicago Press, 2000), 661–65.

37 See Galston, *Liberal Pluralism*, 6.

38 Aristotle, *Nichomachean Ethics*, 318–20.

39 A contemporary viewpoint on these subjects closer to my own than most is advanced by Amitai Etzioni. He maintains that "a good society requires a carefully monitored equilibrium of order and autonomy, rather than the maximalization of either" (*The New Golden Rule* [New York: Basic Books, 1996], 4). This concept of "order" includes moral norms and "virtues." The

terms of equilibrium are thoughtfully articulated, but I do not find in them any unifying principle transcending the duality of social order and autonomy. In other words, if Etzioni's work embodies a unified model of the good, or of the worthy human being, I have failed to see it.

40 Niccolo Machiavelli, *The Prince*, trans. Harvey C. Mansfield (Chicago: University of Chicago Press, 1998), 61.

41 Machiavelli, *The Prince*, 70.

42 Machiavelli was not, of course, the discoverer of this truth. Falsehood in political life, and the reason for it, is a major theme of Plato's *Republic*. See especially the "Noble Lie" at the end of book 3.

43 Machiavelli, *The Prince*, 101.

44 At the time of Pearl Harbor, would it have made sense for our leaders to deliberate about what would constitute moderation in our response to the attack? What is needed in such situations is decisiveness.

45 *From Max Weber: Essays in Sociology*, ed. H. H. Gerth and C. Wright Mills (New York: Oxford University Press, 1958), 115.

46 *From Max Weber*, 115.

47 Weber, *From Max Weber*, 152. This famous passage from Weber resembles the viewpoint from Isaiah Berlin I've cited, supra, 29–31. Or, rather, the latter resembles the former; Berlin seems to have adopted or presupposed the Weberian view that the world is an arena of irreconcilable ideological rivalries. However, they do not draw quite the same conclusion from this perceived reality. Weber does not (as far as I can tell) draw the liberal conclusion that a very accommodating "pluralistic" society is the best one. After all, a society or its leaders could as easily make a decisive choice for theocracy. Perhaps there is a distinction to be made between "softer" and "tougher" versions of moral pluralism.

48 *From Max Weber*, 119–20.

49 Melville, *Billy Budd, Sailor*, ed. Harrison Hayford and Merton M. Sealts Jr. (Chicago: University of Chicago Press, 1962), 76.

50 One can sympathize with the claim that these passions represent deviations from the authentic scriptural teachings, yet it is evident that "holy war" is periodically urged in the Koran, the book of Deuteronomy, and elsewhere.

51 See Søren Kierkegaard, *Fear and Trembling* (London: Penguin Books, 1985).

52 The classical biblical case is the Abraham and Isaac story in the book of Genesis. God demands of Abraham that he sacrifice his beloved son Isaac "as a burnt offering" (Gen 22). As we know, at the last moment, the Lord spares Isaac and promises to heap blessings upon Abraham and his descendants "because you have done this and not withheld your only son." For

some commentators this is biblical religion at its worst, sanctifying blind obedience even to commands that would violate the moral law, family bonds, and compassion. The Kierkegaardian interpretation is more subtle, using the story to illustrate the arduousness, the paradoxes, and even the psychological profundities of genuine faith.

53 Bernard Lewis writes: "The idea that any group of persons, any kind of activities, any part of human life is outside the scope of religious law and jurisdiction is alien to Muslim thought. . . . There is only a single law, the shari'a, accepted by Muslims as of Divine origin and regulating all aspects of human life: civil, commercial, criminal, constitutional" (Lewis, *What Went Wrong?* [New York: Oxford University Press, 2002], 100).

54 Alexis de Tocqueville, *Democracy in America*, ed. and trans. Harvey C. Mansfield and Delba Winthrop (Chicago: Univeristy of Chicago Press, 2000), 2:510–11.

55 This consideration is, I think, the underlying theme of John Locke's *Letter on Toleration*.

56 Court cases in this area are too numerous for useful citation here. As I am writing this, yet another "moment of silence" case seems headed toward the Supreme Court, and "under God" is under litigation.

57 It seems to me that this principle is at the root of Chief Justice John Marshall's affirmation of judicial power to review acts of Congress in *Marbury v. Madison*.

58 Thomas Hobbes, *Leviathan* (London: Collier Books, 1962), 490–91.

59 Aristotle, *Politics*, in *Introduction to Aristotle*, ed. Richard McKeon (New York: Modern Library, 1949), books 3 and 4.

60 Locke, *The Second Treatise of Government* (Indianapolis: Bobbs-Merrill, 1952), 15.

61 Locke, *The Second Treatise of Government*, 54.

62 Locke, *The Second Treatise of Government*, 91–102.

63 While this is an ideal, it is not a dreamy mythology. Often enough our courts have to wrestle with its demands as they encounter conflicting claims of great magnitude—such as those of law enforcement and those on behalf of the rights of persons threatened with criminal punishment, both representing vital desiderata of a decent society. As the eminent Justice Felix Frankfurter has put it, the Constitution's broad provisions on due process of law have placed upon the Supreme Court "the duty of exercising judgment, within the narrow confines of judicial power in reviewing state convictions, upon interests of society pushing in opposite direction" (*Rochin v. California*, 342 U.S. 165, 171 [1952]). Serious recognition that there are

"interests of society pushing in opposite directions" is the hallmark of what I would call a jurisprudence of moderation.

64 Insofar as this essay has relied upon philosophical sources, it can be criticized for insufficient attention to the philosophers most unfriendly to moderation. The unfriendliest of course are Nietzsche and his progeny in postmodernism. For Nietzsche there are no truths—only various "perspectives," and perspectives are products of passions organized (when they are organized) by one's "will to power." See Friedrich Nietzsche, *Beyond Good and Evil* (New York: Vintage Books, 1989), esp. his Preface and parts 1 and 5. On this view impartiality and moderation can only be perspectival fictions—and unworthy ones, for they weaken the will. If you are really alive, what you do and what you write is for the sake of mastery, not truth. But shall we not think critically about the will to power and the claim that thinking is always under its command? To those who still find the case for moderation uncompelling, here is the last argument: consider the alternatives.

Chapter 2

1   *Thus Spake Zarathustra*, in *The Philosophy of Nietzsche* (New York: Modern Library, 1907), 12.

2   *Thus Spake Zarathustra*, 11. Tocqueville anticipated the Nietzschean insight, though rather less harshly. Americans, he said, are typically devoted to "making life easier and more comfortable at each instant, preventing inconvenience, and satisfying the least needs without effort and almost without cost. These objects are small, but the soul clings to them: it considers them every day and from very close; in the end they hide the rest of the world from it, and they sometimes come to place themselves between it and God" (*Democracy in America*, 509). Tocqueville's worry about this materialism was not that it would lead to moral corruption but that its narrow preoccupation with little mundane gratifications could eventually bring about a kind of shrinkage of the soul and low-spirited enervation.

3   Nietzsche, *Beyond Good and Evil* (New York: Vintage Books, 1966), 109.

4   "The discipline thinkers imposed upon themselves to think within directions laid down by a church or court, or under Aristotelian presuppositions, the long spiritual will to interpret all events under a Christian schema . . . all this, however forced, capricious, hard, gruesome and antirational, has shown itself to be the means through which the European spirit has been trained to strength." None of these grand orientations, including the

Christian one, have been grounded upon a rationally defensible understanding of the world, but historically they have "educated the spirit" (Nietzsche, *Beyond Good and Evil*, 101).

5   Nietzsche, *The Philosophy of Nietzsche*, 954.

6   Nietzsche, *The Philosophy of Nietzsche*, 958.

7   Nietzsche, *The Philosophy of Nietzsche*, 1087.

8   Nietzsche occasionally uses that term, and was the first major thinker to do so in the manner later made famous by Freud.

9   Aristotle, *Nichomachean Ethics*, book 6. Perhaps the Aristotelian idea of practical wisdom can get some support from psychological research currently abounding (though much debated) on the concept of "emotional intelligence," a kind of intelligence that draws upon feelings as it channels them. See Daniel Goleman, *Emotional Intelligence* (New York: Bantam Books, 1995).

10   *Nichomachean Ethics*, 346.

11   Plato's Socrates says that the wise man, recognizing the factions, the disparate elements of the soul, "binds them together and becomes entirely one from many, moderate and harmonized" (*The Republic of Plato*, ed. and trans. Allan Bloom [New York: Basic Books, 1968], 123).

12   *Thus Spake Zarathustra*, 11.

13   *Thus Spake Zarathustra*, 24.

14   In *D. H. Lawrence: The Complete Poems* (New York: Penguin Books, 1993), 558.

15   In Ayn Rand's novel *The Fountainhead*, the hero, a stunningly innovative architect, finds the Establishment unwilling to allow his grand construction to be used for the purposes he envisioned, so he dynamites the structure. Thus is vitalistic self-assertion celebrated.

16   See Jean-Paul Sartre, "Existentialism Is a Humanism," an essay sometimes called "What Is Existentialism?" Nietzsche's superior man is the author of his own standards of value. "Canst thou give unto thyself thy bad and thy good and set up thy will as a law over thee?" (*Thus Spake Zarathustra*, 66). But for Nietzsche this is an extraordinary and most arduous exertion; very few of us can do it. For Sartre we can all do it if only we will free ourselves from the self-delusory idea that there are moral guidelines somewhere in the world. Sartre democratizes Nietzsche.

17   *Love Poems of John Donne* (Mount Vernon, N.Y.: Peter Pauper Press), 50.

18   In his most interesting phenomenology of the erotic life, Roger Scruton describes this phenomenon as the "mutual embodiment" of two persons.

See Scruton, *Sexual Desire* (New York: Macmillan, 1986).

19 Here is an appropriate place for this debater's point: if you regard my argument as a mere articulation of the obvious, you cannot also regard it as an arbitrary ideological construct imposed upon reality.

20 Sigmund Freud, *Civilization and Its Discontents* (New York: Norton, 1961), 32–33.

21 Freud, *Civilization and Its Discontents,* 33.

22 Freud, *Civilization and Its Discontents,* 35.

23 That some of our passions lend themselves to the insatiably addictive is one factor, and no small one, in the case for moderation. Consider addictive gambling, power- or reputation-seeking, drug consumption, and, of course, insatiable Eros.

24 In their book *Habits of the Heart*, Robert Bellah and his associates interview a man who says this: "Life is a big pinball game; and you have to be able to move and adjust yourself to situations if you're going to enjoy it" (Bellah, et al., *Habits of the Heart* [Berkeley: University of California Press, 1996], 77). The capacity for adjustment to variable situations is fine up to a point, but on the "pinball game" view of life, all commitments are so tentative that, strictly speaking, you really have no commitments, and in that case who are you? One who has no prominent aspiration or commitment could end up having to admit, like T. S. Eliot's pitiful character J. Alfred Prufrock, that "I have measured out my life with coffee spoons." As the reader of Eliot's poem may discern, the big trouble with a Prufrockian existence is not exactly that it is painful, but that it is empty; it lacks any vital or coherent definition.

25 Nietzsche dissents; I come to that in the next chapter, with regard to his claim that seriousness of purpose requires the limitation of one's horizons.

26 Clearly following from the perspective on moderation I'm offering is that the balancing it recommends does not entail that all the inclinations to be balanced must get equal weight; it does entail that one's "major" shouldn't be all that matters.

27 *Nichomachean Ethics,* 502.

28 Matt 5:43 (*New Oxford Annotated Bible* [New York: Oxford University Press, 1977]).

29 For Freud this condition is not only natural but also just fine, for two reasons: "a love that does not discriminate seems to me to forfeit a part of its own value, by doing an injustice to its object; and secondly, not all men are worthy of love" (*Civilization and Its Discontents,* 57). Indeed, on the Freudian understanding that fiercely hostile and aggressive impulses inhabit our id, how lovable could most of us be?

30 *Nichomachean Ethics,* 504.

31 Jean-Jacques Rousseau, regarded as a philosophic founder of the secular ethic of compassion, seems to make exaggerated claims for it as the root of "all the social virtues." He remarks: "But what is generosity, clemency or humanity but compassion applied to the weak, to the guilty, or to mankind in general? Even benevolence and friendship are, if we judge rightly, only the effects of compassion, constantly set upon a particular object: for how is it different to wish that another person may not suffer pain and uneasiness and to wish him happy?" (Rousseau, *Discourse on the Origins of Inequality,* trans. G. D. H. Cole [New York: E. P. Dutton, 1950], 225). But Rousseau is a notoriously complex and dramatically paradoxical thinker. In his major work of political theory, *The Social Contract,* compassion as such has virtually no role to play in the formation or maintenance of the communal bond.

32 When this was called to their attention, most of my students over the years have wanted to add compassion to the list.

33 "[G]oaded on by the id, hemmed in by the super-ego, and rebuffed by reality, the ego struggles to cope with its economic task of reducing the forces and influences which work on it and upon it to some kind of harmony; and we may well understand, how it is that we so often cannot repress the cry: 'Life is not easy'" (Freud, *New Introductory Lectures on Psychoanalysis* [New York: Norton, 1933], 109). The ego "frequently gives way," but even when it stays in the fight its life is hard.

34 "For man, when perfected, is the best of animals," but "if he have not [acquired] virtue, he is the most unholy and the most savage of animals" (Aristotle, *Politics,* in *Introduction to Aristotle,* 557).

35 Frederick Perls, et al., *Gestalt Therapy: Excitement and Growth in the Human Personality* (New York: Julian Press, 1951), 144–45.

36 Perls, et al., *Gestalt Therapy,* 4–8.

37 Perls, et al., *Gestalt Therapy,* 140.

38 I have noted respects in which the Gestalt perspective is reminiscent of Aristotle, and I will note some respects in which it might remind us of Nietzsche, but it seems to me that the philosophy with which it is most clearly connected is the pragmatism of John Dewey. Consider how prominent is the idea of "growth" (imprecise though it may be) in Dewey's *Human Nature and Conduct* and his writings on education.

39 This can be added: someone easily changeable and variable lacks the inner resources with which to stand up to the opinion of others or to currents

of public opinion; at the other extremity, an excessively resolute person will be, often to his detriment, stubbornly unpersuadable by anyone else. Jane Austen illuminates the dilemma in her novel *Persuasion*. Her heroine, Anne Elliot, reflects upon attitudes of the man she loves. "Anne wondered whether it ever occurred to him now, to question the justness of his own previous opinion as to the universal felicity and advantage of firmness of character; and whether it might not strike him that, like all other qualities of the mind, it should have its proportion and limits. She thought it could scarcely escape him to feel, that a persuadable temper might sometimes be as much in favor of happiness, as a very resolute character" (*Persuasion* [Mineola, N.Y.: Dover Publications, 1997], 87). But any reader can see how the happy reconciliation of Anne and Captain Wentworth is facilitated by the solidity of character which is so fundamental in both cases.

40 Perls, et al., *Gestalt Therapy*, 153.

41 Abraham J. Heschel, *Who Is Man?* (Stanford, Calif.: Stanford University Press, 1965), 28.

42 Goleman, *Emotional Intelligence*, 46.

43 Goleman, *Emotional Intelligence*, 47.

44 Character does seem to be of importance to Goleman, though in his book I can find only this one explicit reference to it: "There is an old-fashioned word for the body of skills that emotional intelligence represents: *character* . . . The bedrock of character is self-discipline; the virtuous life, as philosophers since Aristotle have observed, is based on self-control" (Goleman, *Emotional Intelligence*, 285). But I can't tell whether emotional intelligence is supposed to be identical with character or simply a major instrument in its cultivation. Aristotle could agree with the latter alternative but surely not with the former, and in Aristotle's teaching, wisdom in the practical sense is at least as dependent upon preexisting character as character is upon it- and *that* dependence is not explicitly recognized by Goleman.

45 Critics of or people skeptical about emotional intelligence argue that its proponents have not succeeded in demonstrating its existence on a scientific basis. Of course they haven't. The study of emotional intelligence is not a rigorous science; I think of it as an effort to articulate, with some research support and some difficulties, what practical wisdom concerning the emotional life means. For an elaborate survey of the critical reactions, see Gerald Matthews, Mark Zeidner, and Richard D. Roberts, *Emotional Intelligence: Science and Myth* (Cambridge, Mass.: MIT Press, 2004).

46 Goleman, *Emotional Intelligence*, 56.

47 Intriguingly though the idea of "self" somehow emerges in his *Nichomachean Ethics*, 502; "The good man is related to his friend as to himself (for the friend is another self)." Aristotle's regular terminology, like that of Plato and classical thought generally, is the terminology of "soul." I have employed "self" periodically because (elusive as the concept might be) it performs an individuating function: it designates, as "soul" usually doesn't, the distinctive psyche of a particular individual. Of course, philosophic or scientific materialists tend to reject both terms.

CHAPTER 3

1 Pronouncements of this sort abound in various forms and formats; a more interesting version than most can be found in Michel Foucault, *Discipline and Punish*. Also, some of the more interesting and interestingly problematic formulations are discernible in writings of Stanley Fish.

2 Clifford Geertz, "Anti Anti-Relativism," *American Anthropologist* 86 (1984): 264.

3 Plato's Socrates says: "Isn't it by now plain that it's not possible to honor wealth in a city and at the same time adequately to maintain moderation among the citizens, but one or the other is necessarily neglected?" (*The Republic of Plato*, ed. and trans. Allan Bloom [New York: Basic Books, 1968], 233).

4 Liberal educators can see how this issue has a direct bearing upon classroom teaching. We are currently embroiled in an ongoing debate in the academy about the "indoctrination" of students by teachers who deem it appropriate to use their courses as platforms for the advancement of a political or ideological agenda, especially regarding those subjects in the social sciences and humanities where controversial matters are embedded. Postmodernists don't want to be considered indoctrinators, but they are often found insisting that neutrality among "values" is a manifest impossibility, and that professors purporting to be ideologically impartial are in effect perpetrating a fraud—a biased agenda inevitably lurking beneath claims of impartiality. This line of argument tends to obliterate the distinction between education and propaganda, offering a green light to the latter. Seeking to maintain that crucial distinction, Max Weber, in his essay "Science as a Vocation," laid down the principle that intellectual integrity requires total abstention from moral or political evaluation in the classroom; you must focus on matters of fact or cause and effect and stay away from ethical judgments. But this solution to the problem is itself problematic; much of liberal education

is learning how to think about questions of value by engaging them, and in such engagements absolute professorial neutrality is an unnatural expectation. What can be expected is a classroom atmosphere that encourages serious confrontation with the most thoughtful ideas on all sides, and to that end you want a professor for whom the desideratum of dialogue among opposing viewpoints takes precedence over the advancement of his or her own. This, finally it seems to me, is the agenda of liberal education, and dedication to it is what distinguishes an educator from a propagandist.

5   See, for example, Ronald Dworkin, *Taking Rights Seriously* (Cambridge, Mass.: Harvard University Press, 1977).

6   Nietzsche, *Beyond Good and Evil*, 2.

7   Friedrich Nietzsche, *On the Advantage and Disadvantage of History for Life*, trans. Peter Preuss (Indianapolis: Hackett, 1980), 10.

8   Nietzsche, *On the Advantage and Disadvantage of History for Life*, 11.

9   Nietzsche, *Beyond Good and Evil*, 16.

10 Nietzsche says: "Physiologists should think before putting down the instinct of self-preservation as the cardinal instinct of an organic being. A living being seeks above all to *discharge* its strength—life itself is *will to power*; self-preservation is only one of the indirect and most frequent *results*" (*Beyond Good and Evil*, 21). The "physiologists" think they have objective evidence; does Nietzsche think he does? In view of our main theme, we note that moderation is better served by the former idea than the latter; self-preservation often requires that impulses be moderated, either by the individual or by the laws and rules of a civic community.

11 Nietzsche, *Beyond Good and Evil*, 30–31.

12 Whether in philosophic self-contradiction or not, Nietzsche is a penetrating psychologist of the emotions who evidently wishes us to see certain things as they are: for example, the labyrinthine ways of love, pity, fear, hostility, self-esteem, and their opposites, and our various modes of self-deception. Many of these insights ring true; you cannot dismiss them simply because they constitute neither demonstrable theoretical knowledge nor even practical wisdom in the Aristotelian sense. Undeniably they are, and are meant to be, wisdom of a sort and not just imaginative inventions of the author.

13 Any thoroughgoing exploration of how Nietzsche comes by it would require a lengthy digression from our main theme. Here the following brief suggestions might suffice. If you are persuaded that "values," or ideas of the good and the worthy, are all groundless (because "God is dead") *but* that they are indispensable as inspiration for healthy—that is to say, vigorous—human

endeavors, then it becomes a crucial concern that values be provided some-how—by us. And if you think that reason—the Socratic demand for ratio-nal justification—can only serve to undermine inspirational belief, you are inclined to have recourse to volition; values must be willed into existence and sustained by resolute will. This exertion has to be very resolute espe-cially among those exceptional individuals who are aware of what they are doing, who fully recognize that what they take to be a compelling standard of good and bad is such only because and insofar as they will it to be so. In other words, the man Nietzsche locates at the pinnacle of nobility creates his own horizons, his own order of meanings, knowing that it has no other foundation than that it is his creation. And he judges (and treats) other peo-ple in accordance with the laws dictated by his horizon. Here, succinctly, is the test of nobility: "Cans't thou be judge for thyself and avenger of thy law?" (*Thus Spake Zarathustra*, 66). This is a clarion invitation to immoderation. But Nietzsche deems this necessary as, ultimately, the crucial alternative to an otherwise inevitable nihilism: no beliefs, no values, no inspiration.

14   You are probably glad that the authors of the Declaration of Independence pledged "our lives, our fortunes and our sacred honor" to the principles and purposes enumerated there.

15   See my discussion of this subject in chap. 1, sec. IX, pp. 36–39.

16   If another example of the barbaric is needed, here is one. You are a woman whose brother is suspected of adultery, so the village council decrees that you shall be gang-raped to punish him. Neither civility nor philosophizing can arise from such a cultural milieu.

17   Hobbes writes: "The passions that most of all cause the difference of wit [intelligence] are principally the more or less desire of power, of riches, of knowledge and of honor. All of which may be reduced to the first, that is, desire of power. For riches, knowledge and honor are but several sorts of power" (*Leviathan* [London: Collier Books, 1962], 62). This perception, however, did not prevent Hobbes from considering that he had managed to arrive at objectively valid knowledge of the human condition. The Platonic dialogue most directly devoted to exploration of power and power-seeking is the *Gorgias*.

18   In the dialogue *Meno*, Socrates spins out an analysis showing that nothing can really be known; you cannot understand the whole without truth about the parts, but truths about the parts are unidentifiable without some grasp of the whole. Yet Platonic dialogues proceed to illuminate many subjects despite this intriguing philosophic puzzle.

19 If you are inclined to view this proposition as ethnocentrically Western, consider the many pronouncements of Buddhism—ancient and modern— about "the knowledge of the middle path."

20 Rousseau, *Discourse on the Origins of Inequality,* 210.

21 Rousseau, *Discourse on the Origins of Inequality,* 226.

22 Plato and Aristotle clearly recognized (though they did not emphasize in the manner that Rousseau does) that evils can result from distorted ideation as much as from distorted passion. Socrates saw well enough that false opinions are damaging not only because they stand in the way of truth-seeking, but also because they accompany and nourish irrational affects. That is why the Socratic dialogues relentlessly challenge prominent opinions.

23 Jean-Jacques Rousseau, *Emile,* trans. Barbara Foxley (London: Dent, 1966), 128. This is a central point to which Rousseau returns again and again in *Emile.*

24 Rousseau's imaginary student, Emile, is brought up in the countryside, and his early education is conducted outside of organized society and its influences. *Emile* is an exploration of how far one could be educated so as to retain his natural spontaneity yet also be able to live in modern society. But the precondition of such an education as Emile receives is so stringent as to render it a most unlikely prospect for most of us. While he will eventually learn to use reason, imagination is deliberately unstimulated; at the verge of adolescence "his imagination is still asleep." Rousseau, like Nietzsche after him, recognizes and makes much of the power that imagination holds over our minds and endeavors, and, though distrustful of that power, he (like Nietzsche) is a great employer of it in his own philosophy. Imagination, it would seem, can be a source not only of illusion but also of insights.

25 *Republic of Plato,* 251. Socrates continues with an observation especially remarkable if one has Freud and Nietzsche in mind. He speaks of a "beastly and wild" part of the soul that shows itself in some of our dreams. "You know that in such a state [dreams] it dares to do everything, as though it were released from and rid of all shame and prudence. And it doesn't shrink from attempting intercourse, as it supposes, with a mother or with anyone else at all—human beings, gods and beasts; or attempting any foul murder at all" (251–2). Ancient Greek philosophy was well aware of the Dionysian, though refusing to endow it with all the power that Freud did or the status that Nietzsche gave it.

26 Leon Kass suggests that Rousseau's *Second Discourse* "is, among other things, a remarkable philosophic interpretation of the Garden of Eden story" (Kass, *The Beginning of Wisdom: Reading Genesis* [New York: Free Press, 2003], 60 n.

5). There are indeed striking parallels, although it is doubtful that Rousseau believed in anything approximating the biblical account of Deity. As for the effects of religion in human affairs, Rousseau's writings look at it from two angles—as a fertile source of fanatical strife when untempered, and, when tempered, as an invaluable contribution to moderation.

27 Genesis 11 (*New Oxford Annotated Bible*).

28 This is one of the most remarkable passages in Genesis: "Then Abraham drew near, and said, "Wilt thou indeed destroy the righteous with the wicked? . . . Far be it from thee! . . . Shall not the Judge of all the earth do right?" (Gen 18:23, 25 RSV). What a striking confrontation, especially as it involves one who acknowledges that he is "but dust and ashes"! No inhabitant of Eden could have reached such moral stature or exhibited such human complexity.

29 A horrendous example is offered by Aldous Huxley's *Brave New World*, which portrays the mass production of human beings according to blueprint and by means of a scientifically sophisticated biotechnology.

30 Montaigne, *Complete Essays of Montaigne*, 60.

31 "To the men who told Socrates, 'the thirty tyrants have condemned you to death,' he replied: 'and nature them'" (Montaigne, *Complete Essays*, 64). Montaigne's point is that if you have mastered the fear of death, then you need not be afraid of anything or anyone; you are master of yourself and a free man.

32 As to the determination of one's destiny by mere fate, Shakespeare's *King Lear* says that "men must endure their going hence even as their coming hither; ripeness is all" (Act 5, sc. 1, lines 9–10). Presumably the great philosophic poet didn't mean to suggest that you are without volitional capacity in the determination of your "ripeness."

33 Montaigne, *Complete Essays*, 5.

34 So does Aristotle, in his own way, though Montaigne goes further in this direction.

35 Montaigne, *Complete Essays*, 177.

36 Montaigne, *Complete Essays*, 178.

37 Montaigne, *Complete Essays*, 767.

38 "It would be madness to trust in yourself if you do not know how to govern yourself" (Montaigne, *Complete Essays*, 182). Rousseau, who owes so much to Montaigne, could hardly disagree.

39 This is no place for wrestling with psychological complexities such as this one from Nietzsche: "Whoever despises himself still respects himself as one who despises" (*Beyond Good and Evil*, 81). Whatever Nietzsche might think

of this condition, we may think of it as an example of the intricate patholo-
gies of which the soul is capable.

40 Hamlet says to his friend Horatio: "Give me that man that is not passion's
slave, and I will wear him in my heart's core" (Act 3, sc. 2, lines 69–71).

Conclusion

1 We can also remind ourselves that moderation is not the same thing as
justice (although it often serves well as a prophylactic against injustices).
On the great controversies over slavery, Abraham Lincoln's position was
just and moderate. Henry David Thoreau's position was just, but who could
call Thoreau a moderate? Consider Thoreau's *Civil Disobedience* and *Slavery
in Massachusetts* in comparison with Lincoln's statesmanship on these
subjects.

2 Plato, "Apology," in *Euthyphro, Apology, Crito* (Indianapolis: Bobbs-Merrill,
1948), 49.

3 See Thucydides' *Peloponnesian Wars* on what can happen in a great city
when the norms of civilization collapse.

BIBLIOGRAPHY

Aristotle. *Introduction to Aristotle*. Edited by Richard McKeon. New York: Modern Library, 1947.

———. *Ethics*. In Aristotle, *Introduction to Aristotle*.

———. *Politics*. In Aristotle, *Introduction to Aristotle*.

Austen, Jane. *Persuasion*. Mineola, N.Y: Dover Publications, 1997.

Bellah, Robert N., et al. *Habits of the Heart*. Berkeley: University of California Press, 1996.

Berger, Brigette, and Peter Berger. *The War over the Family: Capturing the Middle Ground*. Garden City, N.Y.: Doubleday, 1983.

Berlin, Isaiah. *Four Essays on Liberty*. London: Oxford University Press, 1969.

———. *The Crooked Timber of Humanity*. Princeton: Princeton University Press, 1990.

Bible. *New Oxford Annotated Bible*. New York: Oxford University Press, 1977.

Burke, Edmund. *Reflections on the Revolution in France*. In *Two Classics of the French Revolution*. New York: Doubleday, 1989.

Charnwood, Lord. *Abraham Lincoln*. Mineola, N.Y.: Dover Publications, 1997.

Churchill, Winston. "Consistency in Politics." In *Thoughts and Adventures*. New York: Norton, 1990.

Clor, Harry M. *Public Morality and Liberal Society*. Notre Dame, Ind.: University of Notre Dame Press, 1996.

Dewey, John. *Human Nature and Conduct*. Mineola, N.Y.: Dover Publications, 2002.

Diamond, Martin. *The Revolution of Sober Expectations: Delivered at Independence Square, Philadelphia, in the House of Representatives Chamber, Congress Hall, on October 24, 1973*. Washington, DC: American Enterprise Institute, 1974.

Donne, John. *Love Poems of John Donne*. Mount Vernon, N.Y.: Peter Pauper Press.

Dworkin, Ronald M. *Taking Rights Seriously*. Cambridge, Mass: Harvard University Press, 1977.

Eliot, T. S. "The Love Song of J. Alfred Prufrock." In *The Major Poets: English and American*. Edited by Gerrit Hubbard Roelofs. New York: Harcourt Brace, 1969.

Etzioni, Amitai. *The New Golden Rule*. New York: Basic Books, 1996.

Federalist, The. New York: Modern Library, 1937.

Foucault, Michel. *Discipline and Punish: The Birth of the Prison*. New York: Vintage, 1995.

Freud, Sigmund. *Civilization and Its Discontents*. New York: Norton, 1961.

———. *New Introductory Lectures on Psychoanalysis*. New York: Norton, 1933.

Galston, William. *Liberal Pluralism*. Cambridge: Cambridge University Press, 2002.

Geertz, Clifford. "Anti Anti-Relativism." *American Anthropologist*, n.s. 86.2 (1984): 263-278.

Gilbert, Martin. *Churchill: A Life*. New York: Henry Holt, 1992.

Goleman, Daniel. *Emotional Intelligence*. New York: Bantam Books, 1995.

Hart, H. L. A. *Law, Liberty, and Morality*. New York: Vintage Books, 1966.

Heschel, Abraham J. *Who Is Man?* Stanford, Calif.: Stanford University Press, 1965.

Hobbes, Thomas. *Leviathan*. London: Collier Books, 1962.

Huxley, Aldous. *Brave New World*. New York: Harper Perennial, 1946.

Jaffa, Harry V. *Crisis of the House Divided*. Chicago: University of Chicago Press, 1999.

Kass, Leon R. *The Beginning of Wisdom: Reading Genesis*. New York: Free Press, 2003.

Kierkegaard, Søren. *Fear and Trembling*. London: Penguin Books, 1985.

Lawrence, D. H. *The Complete Poems*. New York: Penguin Books, 1993.

Lewis, Bernard. *What Went Wrong?* New York: Oxford University Press, 2002.

Locke, John. *John Locke on Education*. Edited by Peter Gay. New York: Teacher's College, Columbia University, 1964.

————. *The Second Treatise of Government*. Indianapolis: Bobbs-Merrill, 1952.

Machiavelli, Niccolo. *The Prince*. Translated by Harvey C. Mansfield. University of Chicago Press, 1998.

Madison, James. See *Federalist, The*.

Marx, Karl. *The Communist Manifesto*. In *Karl Marx: Selected Writings*. Edited by David McLellan. London: Oxford University Press, 1977.

Matthews, Gerald, Mark Zeidner, and Richard D. Roberts. *Emotional Intelligence: Science and Myth*. Cambridge, Mass.: MIT Press, 2004.

Maugham, W. Somerset. *Of Human Bondage*. New York: Penguin, 2007.

Melville, Herman. *Billy Budd, Sailor*. Edited by Harrison Hayford and Merton M. Sealts. Chicago: University of Chicago Press, 1962.

Mill, John Stuart. *On Liberty*. New York: Liberal Arts Press, 1956.

Montaigne, Michel de. *The Complete Essays of Montaigne*. Edited by Donald M. Frame. Stanford, Calif.: Stanford University Press, 1957.

Muravchik, Joshua. "Socialism's Last Stand." *Commentary*, March 2002.

Nietzsche, Friedrich. *Beyond Good and Evil*. New York: Vintage Books, 1989.

————. *On the Advantage and Disadvantage of History for Life*. Translated by Peter Preuss. Indianapolis: Hackett, 1980.

————. *The Philosophy of Nietzsche*. New York: Modern Library, 1907.

————. *The Use and Abuse of History*. Indianapolis: Bobbs-Merrill, 1949.

Perls, Frederick, et al. *Gestalt Therapy: Excitement and Growth in the Human Personality*. New York: Julian Press, 1951.

Plato. "Apology." *Euthyphro, Apology, Crito.* Indianapolis: Bobbs-Merrill, 1948.

———. *The Republic of Plato.* Edited and translated by Allan Bloom. New York: Basic Books, 1968.

Rand, Ayn. *The Fountainhead.* New York: Penguin, 2005.

Rousseau, Jean-Jacques. *A Discourse on the Origins of Inequality.* In *The Social Contract and Discourses.* Translated by G. D. H. Cole. New York: E. P. Dutton, 1950.

———. *Emile.* Translated by Barbara Foxley. London: Dent, 1966.

Sartre, Jean-Paul. *Existentialism and Human Emotions.* New York: Carol Publishing Group, 1990.

Scruton, Roger. *Sexual Desire.* New York: Macmillan, 1986.

Shakespeare, William. *The Complete Works.* Edited by Stanley Wells and Gary Taylor. Oxford: Clarendon Press, 1986.

Thompson, Norma. *The Ship of State.* New Haven and London: Yale University Press, 2001.

Thoreau, Henry David. *Walden, Civil Disobedience, and Other Writings.* New York: W. W. Norton, 2007.

Thucydides. *The History of the Peloponnesian War.* Translated by Benjamin Jowett. New York: Prometheus Books, 1998.

Tocqueville, Alexis de. *Democracy in America.* Edited and translated by Harvey C. Mansfield and Delba Winthrop. Chicago: University of Chicago Press, 2000.

Weber, Max. *From Max Weber: Essays in Sociology.* Edited by H. H. Gerth and C. Wright Mills. New York: Oxford University Press, 1958.

SUGGESTED READINGS

Aron, Raymond. *Thinking Politically: A Liberal in the Age of Ideology.* Edited by Daniel J. Mahoney and Brian C. Anderson. New Brunswick, N.J.: Transaction Publishers, 1997.

Austen, Jane. *Sense and Sensibility.* New York: Vintage Classics, 2007.

Baumann, Fred. "Raymond Aron and Jean-Paul Sartre." In *Political Reason in the Age of Ideology.* Edited by Bryan-Paul Frost and Daniel J. Mahoney. New Brunswick, N.J.: Transaction Publisher, 2007.

Craiutu, Aurelian. "The Virtues of Political Moderation." *Political Theory* 29, no. 3 (2001): 449–68.

Eidelberg, Paul. *A Discourse on Statesmanship.* Urbana: University of Illinois, 1974.

Etzioni, Amitai, ed. *The Essential Communitarian Reader.* Lanham, Md.: Rowman & Littlefield, 1998.

Glendon, Mary Ann. *Rights Talk: The Impoverishment of Political Discourse.* New York: Free Press, 1991.

Grazia, Sebastian de. *The Political Community: A Study of Anomie.* Chicago: University of Chicago Press, 1948.

Mansfield, Harvey C. *Manliness.* New Haven: Yale University Press, 2006.

Niebuhr, Reinhold. *The Children of Light and the Children of Darkness.* Textbook Publishers, 2003.

Oakeshott, Michael. *The Politics of Faith and the Politics of Skepticism.* Edited by T. Fuller. New Haven: Yale University Press, 1996.

Plato. *The Dialogues of Plato.* Vol. 1. Edited by B. Jowett. Introduction by Raphael Demos. New York: Random House, 1937.

————. *Charmides.* In *The Dialogues of Plato.*

————. *Euthyphro.* In *The Dialogues of Plato.*

Steinberger, Peter. *The Concept of Political Judgment.* Chicago: University of Chicago Press, 1993.

Will, George. *Statecraft as Soulcraft: What Government Does.* New York: Simon & Schuster, 1983.

Wilson, James Q. *The Moral Sense.* New York: Free Press, 1993.

Index